GOD

THE ASTROLOGER

SOUL, KARMA AND REINCARNATION
HOW WE CONTINUALLY CREATE OUR OWN DESTINY

GOD
GODDESS

THE ASTROLOGER

SOUL, KARMA AND REINCARNATION
HOW WE CONTINUALLY CREATE OUR OWN DESTINY

Jeffrey Armstrong

TORCHLIGHT PUBLISHING

shifting the paradigm

First printing 2001
Printed in the USA

Cover design by Ania Borysiewicz
Interior design by Christopher Glenn

Published simultaneously in the United States of America and Canada
by Torchlight Publishing, Inc.

Library of Congress Catalog-in-Publishing Data

Armstrong, Jeffrey
        God the astrologer: soul, karma, and reincarnation: how we continually
create our own destiny/ Jeffrey Armstrong
                p.   cm.
        Includes Bibliographical references and index.
        ISBN 1-887089-31-4 (trade pbk.)
        1. Hindu astrology. 2. Vedas—Criticism, interpretation, etc.

BF1714H5 A76 2001
133.5'9445—dc21   00-053242

Attention Colleges, Universities, Corporations, Associations, and Professional Organizations: *God the Astrologer* is available at special discounts for bulk purchases for fundraising or educational use. Special books, booklets, or excerpts can be created to suit your specific needs.

For more information, contact the Publisher:

Torchlight Publishing
PO Box 52
Badger, CA 93603
Telephone: (559) 337-2200
Fax: (559) 337-2354
Email: Torchlight@spiralcomm.net
Web: www.Torchlight.com

Dedication

This book is dedicated to all
seekers of eternal spiritual knowledge.

Acknowledgments

There are many people to thank for making this book possible:
my beloved spiritual master, His Divine Grace
A. C. Bhaktivedanta Swami Prabhupada,
who initiated me into the inner meaning of the Vedas,
my teacher of Vedic Astrology, Jyotisharaj M.K. Gandhi,
who was a pioneer in bringing Vedic Astrology to the West, and
my professors of comparative religion, Donald Nichole and Noel King,
who opened my understanding to all the world's spiritual traditions.

My great love, partner and inspiration, Sandi Graham has lived the
creation of this book with me and given it birth through her
unwavering commitment, management, and dedication.

My long time student and friend Robin Noll
has inspired me for many years with her
devotion and enthusiasm, and thanks
to Paul Noll for his insightful friendship.

My first wife and dear friend, Jennifer Taylor, and
our beautiful daughter, Guenevere, encouraged me and helped
me to hold the vision of this book for many years. My wonderful sister
Amy Armstrong has always believed in me and promoted my vision faithfully.
My parents, Jim and Linda Armstrong, helped with their caring and support.

Special thanks go to Ania Borysiewicz for designing the book
cover and to Petroula Vrontikis for making magic.

Michelle DeAngelis, Larry Mortorff and
Philip di Franco helped
at just the right time;
thank you all.

The valued editors,
typists, and critical readers:
Roy Richard, Beryle Chambers, Brent Ross,
Avar Laland, Bhakti Ananda Goswami, Steffan Omray,
Ron Marinelli, Clinton Jarboe, Robin H. Stuart, Joyanna Anthony,
each contributed in a valuable wayto polish and refine this book. Special thanks
to our publisher Alister Taylor and the talented team at Torchlight, who saw the vision
of the book and brought it into the world. My deepest gratitude goes to all these friends.

There are numerous other people who have given me wisdom, loved or encouraged me and
supported me on the journey that led to this book. I love, bless and thank them all.

Jeffrey Armstrong

Table of Contents

Prometheus

Stealing fire,
A real live wire,
Prometheus angered the gods.
He stole their flame
In a risky game,
To get even, against the odds.
The key is friction,
With truth and fiction,
A torch that gives off light,
The heart must dare
To breathe pure air
And fly alone in the night.
So he struck a deal
With the chariot wheel,
By rubbing his stick on the rim,
While the disk turned around
He dropped straight down,
For the fire now was him.
Then such a flame
Enveloped his name,
The comet Prometheus,
Blazed through the sky
Like a piercing eye,
We saw him and he saw us.
In a dreadful flash,
With a blinding lash,
We took the fearful boon.
Writhing with pain,
We blinked again,
As Prometheus fell in a swoon.
And the gods in rage,
Fashioned a cage
Of chains, on a lonely rock,
Where broken he lay,
As the vultures preyed,
Twisting his gut like a clock.
Now the light he brought,
Which his spirit bought,
Casts a shadow across our soul
And his borrowed plumes
Now light our rooms,
We live in what he stole.
But until we blaze,
He must spend his days
Chained to a rock for us,
For the stolen fire
Was to take us higher
And we are Prometheus.

Jeffrey Armstrong

Introduction

Carl Jung, Vedic Astrology and My Search for Truth

This book is the result of my thirty-year love affair with astrology. It all began in the Sixties when I was studying psychology at Eastern Michigan University. From a very young age, I was interested in philosophical questions about the purpose of life. I had always asked difficult questions of the ministers, rabbis and priests of various religions. I was hungry for answers to questions for which they had no answers. They were all nice enough, but it seemed to me that they were "just doing their job" or were limited to giving very specific dogmatic answers. The fire of inquiry and passion for truth was not in them. Studying psychology and philosophy at the university gave me a similar feeling. In general, it seemed that the academic world had selected a safe and generally agreed-upon curriculum for our education, one heavily slanted toward modern scientific and technological goals, avoiding religion, esoteric truths and controversy.

One of my favorite questions had to do with cause and effect: Do we live only one life or have we had many? The center of that question asks: "Who am I? Why was I born in my particular circumstances? What is the ultimate purpose of life? What is the soul? Who is God? What is God's intention for life? Does the individual continue after death? What is justice? Who created right and wrong? What is the purpose of the laws of Nature? How does Nature operate?"

I would often ask how God could be called loving and yet give everyone only one obviously unfair chance at life and then extinguish or punish them for failing to achieve some unwritten and abstract goal. I never stopped asking difficult questions.

One ray of hope amid the lab rats and IBM punch cards at the university was the writings of the psychologist Carl Jung. Here was an adventurer not afraid to look at divergent world cultures and entertain their exotic thoughts. As I read his works, I discovered him keenly interested in Eastern thought and—of all things—astrology. In fact, near the end of his career he observed that you could know more about a person by calculating his horoscope than by using a stethoscope. I was sure he couldn't mean the horoscopes published as entertainment in the daily papers. I was equally certain that most people with stethoscopes couldn't tell you anything profound about your self.

Why then was this otherwise very intelligent and famous psychologist practicing—no, even worse—promoting astrology? That question became one that I have heard quite often over the last thirty years. Repeatedly, people would ask me: "Why is an intelligent fellow like you an astrologer?" Whereas I asked myself why my otherwise intelligent professors failed to follow Dr. Jung's lead and study astrology.

Unfortunately, neither the Western psychologists, religionists, scientists or philosophers had any new insights about astrology, karma, reincarnation or the rest of my questions. I once proposed an astrological study to my psychology professors. They answered that the government would not be giving any grants for astrology research—now or in the foreseeable future—unless, that is, I could prove some obvious military use.

Thus it was that astrology became my private passion. In my academic work, I completed majors in English Literature, Psychology, History and Comparative Religion. What I observed through my studies was that almost every great thinker who preceded us had some association with astrology. I wondered if perhaps the ancients were mostly fools and we modern thinkers had finally achieved enlightenment, which was the prevailing view among my professors. The other possibility was that, in our rush toward modernity, we had lost sight of some great wisdom that the ancients knew. Because I did not perceive myself to be surrounded by enlightened beings with answers to life's great questions, I went for studying ancient cultures. Besides, if all the thinkers of the past were so ignorant, why do we call studying them "getting an education"?

Now I threw myself into the great ocean of world thought. I began my study of astrology along with any shred of religious, spiritual, and metaphysical thought available from every ancient culture. I exercised my fledgling knowledge for a deeper understanding of the relationship between humans and the cosmos. At last, I began to study ancient thinkers and all the fragments of their thought that have survived.

I also began to observe the planets and stars, something I have continued now for thirty years. That is the basis of science, to observe and try to find correlations between one phenomenon and another. That is also the fundamental premise of astrology, that the movements in the heavens above us are invisibly connected to events on Earth. Like any scientific experiment, there must be a constant and a variable. In astrology the constant is time, measured by the steady movements of the planets and stars. The apparently inexplicable variant is human behavior. How do cause and effect unfold over time, and what are the linkages between the remote cause and the local effects?

I also discovered that the more you study history, the more you see evidence of how much human achievement and learning has been lost. Most of us have been taught names and dates of battles as the primary focus of history. As Donald Nichole, one of my favorite professors, used to say, "In the study of history, there are always two things: what was happening and what was going on." As I stepped outside the limitation of the university circle of thinking, I found myself in the larger universe of culture and knowledge. It became increasingly clear to me that the story of history I had been taught in school was an edited version written for a particular social purpose.

Did you know that the word *curriculum* means *racetrack*? At an even deeper level, I began to see that it was also a "race" track. The victor in warfare writes the history, often to vilify and diminish another race or culture and justify its own actions. The more I looked for truth, the more it eluded me. It was hard to imagine that so many incorrect understandings were woven into accounts presented as the truth by supposedly professional and objective teachers. Eventually I became what I am today, a kind of historical private investigator unraveling the mystery of our past. I knew intuitively that, somehow, astrology was an important piece of that puzzle. I had no idea at the time how true that intuition would prove to be.

Over the years, I came to think of myself as a kind of spiritual archeologist. Why spiritual? Because we have lost our connection to a time in the past when spiritual knowledge was as abundant as information is today. It appeared to me that many scientific enterprises focus on academic facts and external material data. I saw an abundance of data and a deficiency of meaning.

If ours is an information age, thousands of years ago there was a spiritual age. In between there were Dark Ages which erased many of the links to our past, including those links to ancient astronomy and astrology. There was a time within the last ten thousand years, and probably earlier, during which very sophisticated cultures existed. It is true they did not develop science culminating in industry and our current version of technology. Yet it is equally true that they developed astronomy, medicine, language, architecture and religion to levels that are still far beyond our understanding. Ancient does not mean primitive.

I returned to older cultures to retrieve gems of wisdom from the scattered literary ruins that remain. It has led me on a merry chase. Initially, I was led back to the Greek culture of 2,500 to 2,800 years ago. In school, we are taught that this is the starting point, that our Western civilization began with the Greek thinkers Socrates, Plato, Aristotle, and so on. However, the Greeks were late in history compared to the African, Chinese, Egyptian, Babylonian, Indian, and other ancient peoples. In fact, they copied much and invented little.

So I found myself going even further back, before the Greeks. As I studied the history of language, archeology, astrology, medicine and religion, my path kept ending up in India. That ancient land of spices and mystery repeatedly emerged as the place of origin for all human culture. In fact, it is now provable that there is a very direct line of historical and linguistic development from India to European culture.

Perhaps you're wondering how all this relates to astrology, which is where we began and are going. Let me explain by continuing my personal story. I'm sure you have heard the saying "knock and the door will be opened." The corollary is "when the student is ready, the teacher appears." In my case that meant I was a prime candidate for initiation into the Vedic spiritual teachings of India.

The Vedas are a kind of Ph.D. program for anyone interested in the full potential of religious and spiritual understanding. Until recently, it was very rare for Westerners to gain entrance into the secrets of the Vedic religion. For the first time in thousands of years, many of my generation did exactly that. This acceptance took us beyond an academic or intellectual approach to the sacred Vedas and into their very core. As it turned out, this was a necessary first step in order to understand the true place of astrology in the greater universe of thought.

The astrology I first learned was a fragmented hand-me-down from the Greeks. I studied the modern Tropical, or so-called Western, astrology and practiced it for some years. Then I began reading books on Vedic astrology from India. Eventually I found a master of Vedic astrology as it has been practiced for thousands of years. Imagine my surprise when, among other things, I learned the astrology that the West had inherited from the Greeks is no longer properly connected to the stars. In fact, the actual historical zodiac of twelve star-groups is now twenty-three degrees off from the dates currently used by Western astrology! In simple terms, this means you are not the astrological sign you have been told you are. In most cases, you are actually the previous sign. If you think your Sun sign is Aries, you are really Pisces. If you think your Sun sign is Leo, you are really Cancer. The same is true for all the planets.

It also turns out that we are not in the Age of Aquarius, nor will we be for at least four hundred years. Astrology, and in particular the Vedic astrology of India, is the missing link to our understanding of certain key spiritual questions. It also holds the keys to understanding our individual body type, which is one of the lost secrets of medicine. Vedic astrology is also based upon an understanding of certain natural processes that are the basis of right and wrong conduct and the science of ethics. It holds the keys to an understanding of the angelic realm of divine beings who animate material Nature. It explains action, karma, reincarnation, and how Divine justice is ultimately achieved.

I further discovered that the big three religions that arose in the Middle East—Judaism, Christianity and Islam—are missing both a cosmology and a paradigm of sacred material science. If you read the Bible, Torah and Quran, you will not find detailed information regarding how the universe was formed. You will also not find a scientific description of the elements that compose material nature or how they combine to form the world.

This void has been filled in modern times by a materialistic scientific view of the cosmos that is either skeptical of God or outright anti-theistic. Many cosmological and evolutionary theories put forward by scientists are merely speculations based on scanty evidence and capable of many interpretations. However, the atheistic worldviews have been widely accepted and appear on television and in movies as if they were "scientific truth."

In fact, they are new "non-religious religions" which conform to an empty and atheistic worldview that is a reaction against the overly dogmatic and zealous followers of the above three religions. I discovered in the Vedas of India an ancient literature that predates the other major religious texts. The Vedas present both a theistic religious worldview and a detailed cosmology—an extremely scientific model of how matter is created, maintained and destroyed.

The greatness of modern science and technology is that it has gathered an unprecedented amount of information about how matter works. Its weakness has been in denying the obvious. The obvious truth of our universe and existence is that we and the universe were designed by and are supported by a purposeful and Divine intelligence. The universe is a work of art and great invention, and God is the great artist and inventor responsible for its being. That is not dogma; it is intelligent observation. All true religions share the experience of God's intelligence pervading the creation as the laws that make it work.

However, not all religions have information about the details of how the Divine intelligence carries out justice in the realm of matter. The Vedic view of cause and effect extends "every action has an equal and opposite reaction" to its ultimate conclusion. According to the Vedic view, the laws of nature are a judicial system that is presided over by intelligent beings who are agents of the Supreme Godhead. We, the actors in this world of matter, are all eternal souls who are continually given feedback or reactions to our actions. Those reactions manifest from life to life, even though their origin is forgotten by us. What goes around comes around.

According to Vedic astrology, at the moment of birth the positions of the stars and planets are a kind of score card or electronic sign in the sky. Properly understood, they contain the mysteries of our past, as well as results that are due to happen in the future. The laws of matter and its endless combinations are included in this purposeful view of cause and effect.

The many things I learned all pointed in one direction: God is the original astrologer. The Supreme Person has engineered a realm of unconscious matter where we the eternal souls may come to experience our individuality. That realm is managed by angelic beings, or Devas, who administer cause and effect. Since we are eternal souls, we reincarnate in matter and continue to receive the reactions to our previous actions. The stars at the moment of birth reveal the destiny we have previously created through free will. All of this is orchestrated by God the Astrologer.

In short, I discovered that astrology is not about fortune-telling but, as Carl Jung suspected, it is deeper than psychology and is at the very basis of medicine. True astrology is the missing link between religion and science. If that sounds like a very different definition of astrology than you have previously understood, read on as I try to share my discoveries of how God's Divine Plan is revealed through an understanding of Vedic astrology. To quote William Shakespeare, "There are more things in heaven and earth than are dreamed of in thy philosophy, Horatio."

For the moment, pretend you never heard of astrology, and come with me to the ancient temple of the heavens that existed before the pyramids or ancient Rome were built. Let us follow the lines of starlight as they descend to become the living fabric of our lives. Welcome to the inner sanctuary where the mystical language of the heavens is unveiled.

Universe One to Ten

Love in the name of desire becoming need,
Three blessed children of unrefined light,
Born when lonely Cosmos cast His seed
Into the waiting womb of the Queen of Delight.
Pleasure, alone, drunken on soma and wine,
Red pulsing mountains tossed their molten spue,
Plunged in rushing torrents to the sea,
Thrusting skyward, rock in a jagged line,
Changing the sky to purple, the waters to blue,
A yellow spark in the black of eternity.
Three in time, from the One, started out a pair,
Aching with hunger, for form and solid state,
Burst from the cracks in space sprang forth the Air,
Two locked as one in a circle begin to mate.
Red rushing, blue falling, spinning yet out of sight,
Shuddering violently, broken from end to end.
One downward, one upward,point out and base to base,
Flashed a blinding beginning incredibly bright
Then suddenly breaking in pieces began to blend,
Standing as shadows, reflecting another embrace.
Two thus divided, emerged once again as four,
Balanced with secret desire the star came alive.
Unseen and encompassing,nothing then added one more,
Time, in the silent beginning, the middle was five.
Life-giving lotus, sprung from a bottomless lake,
Navel and nave to the spiraling dance of the seven,
This is the paradox, turning a blazing wheel.
Fountains revolving in concert will finally make
A fabric immortal, bright blueprintof starry heaven.
Streams flowing downward to life, recreating the real.
Nine, now mysterious sphere of reflected dreams,
Shape-shifting parody, lamp in the comfortless night,
Priest of illusions, playing the princess it seems,
Opened the palette of colors, pretending in white.
Love and desire, with need rising once again,
Waving at life dressed in rainbows, appearing free.
Swift-moving mansion, home of the recently dead.
Hidden inside the busy pretensions of ten,
Entangled in images, caught in infinity—
Earth from the one descended, blue, yellow and red.

Jeffrey Armstrong

Chapter One

Cowboys, Indians and Non-Existent Hindus

Do you remember the stereotyped cowboy and Indian films which first came out of Hollywood? If all you knew about the culture of the First Nations were those films, how close would your impressions be to reality? Do you think that the most informed First Nation leaders were brought in as consultants to make certain their culture and viewpoint were properly represented? How about Afro-American culture? Do you think white filmmakers of those days were trying to fairly represent the emotions of people who were descended from slavery? Not very likely!

I remember my experience with this when I went to work in the Middle East on behalf of Apple Computer. I formed very close friendships with my Arab hosts, which allowed me to see their reactions to Americans whose views of Middle Eastern culture were formed by watching Hollywood movies. I can still see them wince as some uncultured American would slap them on the back and say something like, "Hey Abdullah, you guys sure do have a lot of sand here; say, where's your camel parked?"

Abdullah, whose real name is Hammed Nasser and who has a Ph.D. from Oxford, is dealing with another product of the media generation, educated by stereotypes and misinformation. The truth is, Christian, Judaic and Islamic cultures have been at war for over a thousand years; mutual understanding has been the casualty. Scholars of religion sometimes call them "the three ugly sisters" because they all have the same father but can't stand each other. This means their leaders have not been making much effort to study and teach each other's spiritual views. On the contrary, they have been fighting a war of words and guns for a thousand years. It has been a war of beliefs, but more often, a war of greed disguised as a war of beliefs. The net result has been that even supposedly educated people have been taught mostly propaganda regarding the enemy rather than the "enemy's" view of their own teachings. In a colonial culture, the people whose land we just stole are, by definition, the enemy.

One of my favorite cartoons shows a retirement-age American couple, dressed in pith helmets, khaki shorts and dark sunglasses. They are in an open market surrounded by brown-skinned people in native dress. The woman turns to the man and says, "George, have you ever seen so many foreigners in one place in all your life?" The point is, until recently, we have judged most cultures of the world through books written by scholars with a white colonial Judeo-Christian bias. In this book I propose to share some very profound knowledge given to the people of India thousands of years ago. In order to give that knowledge a fair hearing, you will need to resist thinking you already understand India based on stereotypical Hollywood images.

There Is No Such Thing as Hinduism

In modern times, the spiritual thought of India has been called Hinduism. Throughout the world, otherwise learned people discuss "Hinduism." In fact, there is no such thing as Hinduism. The word Hindu is a Persian mispronunciation of the

Sindhu River. The Persians called those people living across the river (now Indus) "Hindus". If the people of India had had a choice, they would not have been called Hindus. It is the name given to them by their conquerors. The correct term for the people of India is the residents of "Bharat Varsha." Bharata was a great king thousands of years ago and *varsha* means land, place or continent. The spiritual tradition of Bharata (India) comes from a collection of books written in a language called Sanskrit. Those books are called the Vedas. So-called Hindus are in fact followers of the Vedas.

Unless you are a student of world culture, you may be asking why this matters and how it relates to astrology and higher understanding, which is our theme. As I said, we haven't always been given the truth about world history; we have been given the victor's propaganda. You see, my simple search to understand astrology, which was, after all, a part of my original search to know the truth about who we are through psychology, led me back in history to find out whose story to believe. Perhaps "his story" is just that! What about "her story," and what about "their story?" ("They" being all the other cultures on our planet.) Where do they say we come from? Even more important, what treasures of wisdom have been buried and lost in the warfare of 3,000 years? My movement toward the stars led me down a trail of historical breadcrumbs left by every ancient culture. As it turns out, astrology/astronomy is one of the oldest and universally practiced sciences on our planet. Originally, it was not separate from either religion or science, and neither were our ancient ancestors separate from one another.

There Was No Aryan Invasion

Why India (Bharata) then? The answer to that question is going to amaze and perplex you. It is twofold: The first part is that Bharata is the oldest surviving ancient culture with a written record and living tradition of its ancient knowledge. The most recent archeological evidence now proves that the Bharata culture is at least ten thousand years old. It is also now conclusively proven that this culture arose in India. There was no so-called Aryan invasion of India from the north or anywhere else. This means that the most complete record of ancient history exists in and originated in the Vedic literatures. Two of those Vedas are the Mahabharata and the Ramayana. These are epic poems of over 40,000 and 100,000 verses, respectively. They are written in Sanskrit, which is now universally acknowledged by all linguists to be the parent language of Greek, Latin, and most European languages.

The best known Vedic literature is the Bhagavad-gita, which is a mere 700 verses from the Mahabharata. In addition to the epics, there are four original Vedas: the Rik, Sama, Yajur and Atharva, each of which are thousands of verses in length. In addition, there are 108 Upanishads, each the size of a small novel. Then there are 18 Puranas, which are a kind of religious history and cosmology all in one. These range from ten to seventy thousand verses in length. These are the primary texts of the Vedic spiritual tradition. In addition, there are six *vedangas*, or supporting disciplines, and thousands of explanatory books that expand and classify the meaning of the Vedas. This is by far the largest body of ancient or modern spiritual knowledge on our planet.

Sanskrit, the Perfect Language

In simple terms, this means Bharata is the historical home of what was to become Western civilization, including the Greek and Roman cultures. Instead of only teaching Latin, Greek, and the epics The Iliad and The Odyssey, all universities should begin both historical education and literature with a study of Sanskrit and the Vedas. In the future, students of literature, language and history will find Sanskrit and its literatures at the top of their reading list. If you study the origin of words in English, they lead back through the European languages to Latin, to

Greek, and then to Sanskrit. The final Sanskrit grammar was published by the year 500 BCE. Think of Sanskrit as a spiritual programming language that was used for preserving accurate information over long periods of time. It has been used for thousands of years to transmit ancient knowledge, including astronomy, mathematics and astrology.

To make a comparison, imagine that Microsoft came out with a version of Windows that was so perfect that there was no need for an upgrade for 2,500 years! Once this treasure of ancient Vedic knowledge is properly understood by scholars, then hopefully they will overcome ego, national pride and religious bias to learn whatever secrets are hidden there. As we continue to reassemble the historical puzzle, pieces will be contributed by various cultures only if we can remove the fears that block transmission of their knowledge. After all, the purpose of education is to find as much of the truth as possible.

Picture yourself in the position of all the older cultures that were dominated, damaged, and often ruined by modern conquerors whose primary interest was exploitation. Would you be inclined to reveal your deepest, most intimate secrets to the person who just stole your belongings, raped your women, and burned your house down? It should not come as a surprise that most of the literature written about cultures like Bharata has been written by scholars outside that tradition who often had their own private agendas or were not educated in the secret meaning of the Vedas.

Post-Colonial Revelations

Conversely, the search for truth would not be served by superficially becoming a neo-Hindu just because there is great knowledge in the Vedas. Current India is not always a role model for the living truth of the Vedas, but modern India is nonetheless the living remnant of a once great civilization that gave rise to much of world culture. More importantly, India is still the repository of important knowledge that has not yet been totally revealed to the rest of the world.

This book is the result of an historical process. I, and others like me, have now been allowed to enter the actual temple of ancient Indian spiritual truth and have come back to report to you of what we found there. We, who are the descendants of the conquerors, are now being trusted to enter the inner sanctum of a sacred place that has been carefully protected for ten thousand years. Much of the knowledge in this book existed, as you will learn, before the pyramids were built.

In fact, the pyramids were built with a perfect alignment to the stars because many of the great ancient cultures had a profound understanding of astronomy/astrology. They also understood the spiritual significance of the stars and planets in our lives as the intermediary between the spiritual realm and the manifest material world. Because of Sanskrit, modern-day India just happens to be one of the few remaining representatives of that ancient age with a written record and active memory of that once great past.

Often people ask me why I study the knowledge of India when the culture there is filled with problems. My answer is a comparison. Picture a ninety-year-old man who was once an Olympic runner jogging down the sidewalk when a young teenage boy races by. As he passes him, he says, "Hey old man, how come you run so slow? Don't you know to exercise?" What can the older man say? Perhaps in time the young man will be ready to sit and listen to his wisdom. It reminds me of something Mark Twain once said: "When I was eighteen my parents were really stupid. It was amazing how much they had learned by the time I was twenty-three." This book is filled with wisdom from very ancient voices. Please don't confuse the old body (which is India today) with the great wisdom from a wise and ancient culture.

Circle of Light

Om Namo Bhagavate Vasudevaya

Circle of light, revolving endlessly in space,
Shaping with subtle beams the lines of every face,
As above, so below, each action finds its place.
Projected from another plane, desire sped,
Bursting origin of fire, smoldering red,
Deep crack from the mines of doom in the cosmic head.
This evolved into a power fair, songs that rejoice,
The word broke free and sang, the day a shinning voice,
Left and right turning neck, paradox wisdom's choice.
To live and living divide the One to sexes,
Clever fingers braid three strands, a twisted nexus,
Information aped the brain, churning complexes.
Breast of heaven, pearled orb, swift mother of fate,
Two solidified as four, fluid Southern gate,
Home and haven, medicine, kindness conquers hate.
Bright heart, the pyramid, to focus every ray,
Offspring of light, born on the lotus, truth to say,
Lion in the night, golden, roaring forth as day.
Hidden, yet open, the virgin where none suspect,
Soft spot, decision, daily learning to protect,
This craftsman building bright new worlds with intellect.
Conflict to culture grows; love is the highest law,
Dancing rainbows, blind on the canvas, what she saw
Lives in dreams, I am many, we must learn to draw.
Deep desire burns death, dark immortality,
This secret seed will grow into eternity,
Death to life, dying clings with great tenacity.
Now the vision, man breaks forth, eyes upon the goal,
Every star is truth in fragments, a greater whole
Calls answers, food to feast, the beast now serves the soul.
Dark light where all is shadow, time to wake the spore,
Triumph, wisdom, slave to logic's law, peace or war,
Father-time, master, watching at the unknown door.
Future peace, which hangs upon the universal,
Listening to inner voices, who will heed the call?
To understand the circle must include us all.
Dreams, now visions turning, the whole is in each part,
There in the universe, which is the human heart,
End and beginning, right before another start.
Bright Circle of Light, reaching out its lines to trace
Designs of infinity, on the human face,
As above so below, each action filled with grace.

Om Namo Bhagavate Vasudevaya

Jeffrey Armstrong

Chapter Two

Astrology Was the First Science

When I began my study of astrology, I didn't understand it would lead me back into ancient history. I certainly had no idea of its true nature or potential. Like most people, I was interested in me. What is my sign? What does it say about me? This is the appeal of the daily horoscope. People are impatient to hear the part about themselves. "Get to the point" and "give me the bottom line," they say. I will, but first there are some important pieces of the cosmic puzzle that I need to share with you. To do that we need to look at some basic astronomy and ancient history. The secret hidden in astrology is much more profound than just our personal horoscopes.

Originally, there was no separation between astrology and astronomy. What could be more natural than to study the Sun, Moon, planets and stars? Our ancestors watched the sky at night the way we now watch television. They noticed that the seasons of the year followed the movements of the Sun and Moon. Since time is cyclic, they learned to predict the return of each season and thus the timing of rains and warmth or cold that were essential to growing food or for navigation when traveling. They saw the stars in elegant patterns that appeared to them as meaningful shapes. It was as if the shapes of the constellations were telling a story.

Those groups of stars were given names and used for navigation. Their fixed arrangements were also perceived as part of a greater mystery, the secret of our origin and place in the Cosmos. The signs of the zodiac—Aries, Taurus, Gemini, Cancer, Leo, Virgo, Libra, Scorpio, Sagittarius, Capricorn, Aquarius and Pisces—are groupings of the stars visible in the Northern Hemisphere. That belt of stars extends to approximately 8° either side of the ecliptic (Earth's planar path around the Sun). There were also the visible planets, Mercury, Venus, Mars, Jupiter and Saturn, that move in their orbits upon that plane and thus through the starry belt of the zodiac situated behind, each at different speeds. In recent times there are also the newly discovered outer planets, Uranus, Neptune and Pluto.

You could say that astronomy and astrology are both studying the light of the universe. Since both a visible and an invisible reality always surround us, there is always an objective and subjective side to everything that exists. For example, the visible light we see through our eyes is objective. In fact, that is how we see objects—with visible light. The light of thought—memory and imagination—is subjective. Energies like x-rays or microwaves are also real but to our normal perception they are invisible. Now that modern science has proven the existence of so many invisible realities, it is much easier to understand how ancient thinkers looked at the light of the Cosmos and intuitively saw that it was influencing us in ways that were not immediately obvious. It is for this reason that you could think of astronomy as the study of the objective reality of the stars and astrology as the science of the invisible meaning of those objective observations.

Something Invisible Is Changing

Another way to think of this is illustrated by the relationship between the body and mind. No one has ever seen a mind in the same objective way they see a body. Yet everyone sees and accepts the influence of the mind. In medicine, this is called the psychosomatic/somatopsychic relationship. Whatever happens to the body affects the mind and whatever occurs in the mind affects the body. The basis of astrology is like that. We live in the Cosmos, surrounded by varying patterns of energy. We are in the Cosmos but the Cosmos is also in us. The changes in the objective positions of the stars and planets are an indication that something invisible is also changing. In that sense, you could say that astrology is the study of our invisible relationship to cosmic energies and intelligence.

Take the example of a sunspot. Before satellites and electronic communication, a sunspot might never have been objectively noticed on Earth. It could barely be seen with the unaided eye. Now that we have electronic devices in space, when there is a solar eruption we can measure the energy. That same energy which was invisible to us in the past can now be measured. Yet at the cellular level that blast of energy will affect us in either case, whether we see it or not. So our relation to all of life is, and always has been, both objective and subtle (or invisible).

Our knowledge of the physical universe can be likened to the body, whereas astrology is more like the mind. It is interesting that the modern scientific revolution, which has so successfully mapped the objective, has also accidentally validated the subjective (or invisible) to a much greater degree. The quest for objective knowledge has led to the unseen just as surely as the unmanifest leads to the physical. In astrological terms this is stated: "As above, so below." Everything in the universe is interconnected. We live in the Cosmos and are a product of it, subject

31

to the same laws; therefore we are a small universe, or microcosmos.

Of course, in modern times, astrology has generally been presented as entertainment. The daily horoscopes in the paper are mostly that. Nevertheless, to their credit, they do serve as a reminder that we have an ongoing relationship with the universe. That is a step in the right direction. It would be fair to say that during the last centuries of scientific revolution and invention, we have become overly preoccupied with the physical and objective. The benefits of that focus are obvious to us all, as are some very serious imbalances that remain to be dealt with. I would suggest that part of that imbalance arose from the pushing aside of many spiritual and subtle aspects of our being. In that sense, science is really a new religion which has aggressively pushed aside old forms of thinking as if they were rivals. Many people have come to think that if you are logical or scientific, you can not at the same time be psychic or spiritual; but I would say that, too, is a limitation. Why not develop both intuition (spiritual understanding) and logic?

Acausal Synchronicity

In this way, astrology was gradually pushed into a corner for not being "scientific." It just appeared too unbelievable that stars and planets could influence us from such great distance. However, scientific minds are now beginning to entertain the wisdom of the great thinkers of ancient times. When you realize that most of the philosophers, rulers and scientists of past times were certain that astrology is genuine, it cannot be dismissed so easily.

In another quote, psychologist Carl Jung had an interesting comment on this point: "Because I am a scientist, I must tell you that I have observed a synchronicity between the movement of points of light in space and events on Earth. Because I am a scientist, I cannot tell you for certain why it is so. Therefore, I call astrology *acausal synchronicity.*" The bottom line is, somehow or another everything in the Cosmos is interconnected.

To understand astrology it is necessary to have a basic grasp of astronomy. The horoscope which an astrologer casts and uses to understand a person's destiny is actually a picture of the sky surrounding the Earth at the moment of birth. *Horoscope* means *view of the hour.*

As you will see, the horoscope is not just your Sun sign but includes other planets and the constellations or star groups as well. A proper understanding of astronomy will also make it clear how Western, or Tropical, astrology is currently using calculations that are separated from the stars by 23º and therefore almost 2,000 years out of date!

The first astronomical reality of importance in this discussion is that the Earth is traveling around the Sun in an elliptical orbit. This gives rise to our experience of the year cycle. Not all the ancients understood that it is the Earth that revolves around the Sun, since it appears that the Sun revolves around Earth. The Vedas do mention that the Sun is the center of the universe in a very old text called the *Rig-veda*, which is at least 8,500 years old. The path of the Earth around the Sun is called the ecliptic. The equator, which divides the Earth in halves at the middle, would be the same as the ecliptic if the Earth's poles were at right angles to the ecliptic. Instead, Earth is tilted in space at an angle of 23½º. Therefore, the ecliptic and equator are different by 23½º.

This tilt gives rise to the changing of seasons which is experienced at northern and southern latitudes. At the equator, there are no seasons because the amount of sunlight does not vary throughout the year. Since Earth is tilted in relation to the Sun, we receive varying amounts of sunlight throughout the year in the northern and southern latitudes. Because the light available to us is always changing, we experience the various seasonal changes.

The longest night of the year is the winter solstice. The first day of spring is the vernal equinox, where day and night are equal but day is growing longer. The longest day of the year is the summer solstice. The first day of autumn, when day and night are equal but day is growing shorter, is the autumnal equinox. We could have chosen any one of those four as the beginning of a new year cycle, but since vegetation returns in spring, it came to be used as the beginning point of each new year.

For the purpose of our discussion, think of the first day of spring, which is usually about March 21st, as a point of focus for this discussion of our relationship on Earth to the Sun, Moon, planets and stars. The other thing to remember is that on Earth everything in space appears to be revolving around us. This means every day the Sun appears to rise and set, when in fact it is the Earth turning once on its axis. Because Earth is tilted 23½°, the place in space where the upper pole of Earth points is experienced by us as north. In other words, we experience the directions north, south, east and west because Earth stays in a particular angular relationship to the Sun and in the background are the fixed stars.

Circle of Seasons, Circle of Animals

Again, our daily experience is that the Sun rises in the east and sets in the west. When the Sun sets, we can then see the rising of the stars and the Moon as well as whatever planets are visible on that particular night. During the day the light of the Sun is too bright for us to see the stars and planets in the sky. It appears to us that everything is rising and setting on a path in the sky. They rise at a place in the east and set at a place in the west. That path is in fact the ecliptic, Earth's path around the Sun. It is called the ecliptic because it is the line on which eclipses of the Sun and Moon take place. Certain groups of stars also appear to rise and set each day. If you imagine a belt of stars 8° either side of that ecliptic, that circle of stars is called the *zodiac*, which in Greek means *circle of animals*.

Since the total circle is 360º, the star groups were divided into groups of approximately 30º, making 12 groups of zodiacal signs. These star groups were eventually named Aries, Taurus, Gemini, Cancer, Leo, Virgo, Libra, Scorpio, Sagittarius, Capricorn, Aquarius and Pisces. These star groups, or constellations, rise and set each day over a period of 24 hours, which means each one is on the eastern horizon for a period of approximately 2 hours, though in fact the time for each varies somewhat. When we are born, the time of birth combined with the latitude and longitude of the place of birth tells the astrologer which of the 12 star groups was rising in the east at that moment. That is called the *rising constellation*, or *rising sign*.

You may be thinking this is only important information for astronomers, that it is not relevant to your daily life. But what if the incoming cosmic rays are a kind of weather that is bombarding us all the time? What if those incoming waves of invisible energy are constantly washing over us and creating predictable effects? What if we are sandwiched in between the magnetism and weather of Earth and the incoming patterns of energy from space? That would make the science of astronomy important in a profound way. The positions of the celestial bodies would be a source of observed patterns of light that could be studied for effects or relationships of correlation within the biosphere of Earth. Either as patterns, which indicate significance, or as sources of cosmic energy, this would be important to understand.

In other words, these patterns would lead to a true application of astrological theory. So come with me on the next step in this journey of understanding. When I made the transition from being a Western, or Tropical, astrologer to a Vedic astrologer, I learned about something called the precession of the equinoxes and that changed everything in my search for our link to the heavens.

The Mermaid's Tail

The unseen mill which grinds us slow
Turns around us and within,
Creating what we think we know—
Retrograde equinoctial spin.
In the ocean, on the floor,
Time is warped and winding down,
The changing Pole Star is the door,
Opening and closing without a sound.
The snake is twisted, dark and light
Have grabbed it by the head and tail,
Churning a milky path through night,
Up the Tree of Life they scale.
Wobbling wheel, the carousel,
Grinding salt beneath the sea,
Seven sages speak but will not tell
The secret shared between the three.
Veiled in mist she bends above,
Wearing bangles sparkling bright,
Dancing slowly in her love,
Turning on the wheel of her delight.

Jeffrey Armstrong

Chapter Three

The Trouble with Earth's Wobble

If there were no other motions of the Earth to consider, the same stars would rise at the same place and time every year. Take for example the first day of spring, March 21st. Every year on that day, the duration of day and night are equal. The Sun rises in the morning on that day, and although its light is too bright for us to see them, the Sun is surrounded by a particular group of stars. Surrounded by means that the stars are there in the background and the Sun appears in their midst. To make this easier to see, let us imagine the Moon is full on that very day.

The Moon revolves around the Earth. New Moon is the time when the Moon appears in the same part of the sky as the Sun. You could think of *New Moon* as "no Moon," since because of its proximity to the Sun, it is not visible to us. In other words, it rises and sets with the Sun; so, we cannot see the Moon. Full Moon is the opposite time of the lunar cycle, when the Sun and Moon appear 180º apart. It is always the case on Full Moon that the Sun sets and the Moon rises at the same moment because they are opposite each other.

Imagine it is Full Moon on the first day of spring. The Sun always rises and sets in a particular star group and at sunset the Moon rises in the opposite star group. The difference is we can see the stars that surround the Moon. Both the Sun and Moon appear in one of those star groups; in other words, they are in a constellation. In this case, they are opposite each other; so, of course, they are in opposite constellations.

The question is: Which star group is the Sun in on March 21st? Is it always in the same constellation or is it gradually changing? If the Earth did not have any other regular motions, the Sun would always be in the same group of stars on March 21st. However, there is one more motion which changes everything.

The Earth Has a Wobble

To understand this other motion of the Earth, picture a top in space orbiting around the Sun once in a year. Picture it revolving or turning on its own axis once in a day. Now imagine that the North Pole of the top has a very slow wobble. If there was a pencil sticking out of the North Pole of the top, for every wobble the pencil would draw a circle in the sky above the top. In the case of our Earth, one wobble takes about 25,920 years. This means that the Earth actually shifts in relation to the fixed stars.

There are two visible results from this shift. The first is a gradual change in the Pole Star. Our current Pole Star, Polaris, is less than 1º from true north. In the year 150 BCE, it was 12º 24 minutes from it. It was not until the fifteenth century that Polaris could be used for navigation as an indicator of true north. As a result of this wobble, Polaris is now gradually ceasing to be our Pole Star. In 13,000 years, the star Vega will be our new Pole Star. When the pyramids were built, the Pole Star was Alpha Dracaenas.

The other result of this wobble is called the precession of the equinoxes. The Earth is changing its relation to the fixed stars. Instead of the same group of stars being with the Sun on the first day of spring, it changes slowly over time. That slow motion causes the first day of spring to precede backward through the zodiac. That means the vernal equinox occurs in one constellation for about 2,160 years. That period of time is referred to as an Age. Right now, we are in the Age of Pisces. This means that on the first day of spring, March 21st, the Sun rises in the constellation of Pisces; today, in the year 2000, it is approximately at 6° of Pisces. Approximately every 72 years, Earth's wobble causes the next degree to cross the vernal equinox, on March 21st.

The movement is backward through the signs of the zodiac. It is a sort of backward cosmic countdown. We started the Age of Pisces around 1,750 years ago when, on the first day of spring, the rising of the Sun occurred in 30° of the constellation Pisces. Over the years it became 29°, 28°, 27°, 26°, 25°—all the way down to today where, on the vernal equinox, the Sun is in 6° of Pisces. Over the next few hundred years, the countdown will continue—5°, 4°, 3°, 2°, 1°—until one March 21st the Sun will no longer be in Pisces but will be in 30° of Aquarius. On that day, over 400 years from now, we will actually enter the Age of Aquarius.

The Premature Age of Aquarius

Yes, I know, the song was done and the mugs and T-shirts are ready and it's the Millennium and all, but the real Age of Aquarius is an astronomical event that will not be happening for at least 400 years. While we are on the subject, it is not really the year 2000 either. No one can agree on the actual year or month of Christ's birth; therefore, 2000 AD (Anno Domini: in the year of our Lord) is purely a made-up number.

Now, back to our discussion about the precession of the equinoxes. Right now we are in the Age of Pisces with four hundred years to go. The previous age was the Age of Aries (2,160

Your Sun Sign

Sidereal*		Western	
April 15 - May 15	Aries	March 21 - April 19	Aries
May 16 - June 15	Taurus	April 20 - May 20	Taurus
June 16 - July 14	Gemini	May 21 - June 21	Gemini
July 15 - Aug. 17	Cancer	June 22 - July 22	Cancer
Aug. 18 - Sept. 17	Leo	July 23 - Aug. 22	Leo
Sept. 18 - Oct. 18	Virgo	Aug. 23 - Sept. 22	Virgo
Oct. 19 - Nov. 17	Libra	Sept. 23 - Oct. 23	Libra
Nov. 18 - Dec. 16	Scorpio	Oct. 24 - Nov. 21	Scorpio
Dec. 17 - Jan. 14	Sagittarius	Nov. 22 - Dec. 21	Sagittarius
Jan. 15 - Feb. 13	Capricorn	Dec. 22 - Jan. 19	Capricorn
Feb. 14 - March 15	Aquarius	Jan. 20 - Feb. 18	Aauarius
March 16 - April 14	Pisces	Feb. 19 - March 20	Pisces

* Date ranges vary annually; consult your sidereal
astrologer for your birth year's ranges

years before Pisces) and before that the Age of Taurus (another 2,160 years earlier). In the Age of Taurus, whoever was born on March 21st had Sun in Taurus. In the Age of Aries, anyone born on March 21st had the Sun in Aries.

Now in the Age of Pisces, anyone born on March 21st has Sun in Pisces. Why is it then that Western (Tropical) astrologers say that someone born on March 21st is an Aries, when that has not been true for 1,750 years?

Old Sign in a New Bottle

Imagine you have a wine bottle, which once held a wine called Aries 1,750 years ago but now holds a wine called Pisces. Would you call the new wine Aries since the bottle used to hold that wine? Similarly, the first day of spring used to be in Taurus for 2,160 years, then in Aries for 2,160 more; but neither of those wines is in the bottle now. The bottle is March 21st and this year the wine in the bottle is Pisces. This means that on March 21st, 2000, the person born is a Pisces. The Sun rose in Pisces on that day and Full Moon would have been in the opposite sign of Virgo.

The person would not be an Aries and the Sun will not be in Aries on that date for another 23,000 years. When the Aquarian Age finally does begin, on March 21st the person born will not be a Taurus, an Aries or a Pisces but rather a Sun in Aquarius. To put it very simply, Western (or Tropical) astrologers are currently acting as if the Aries wine is still in the bottle but it is not and has not been for 1,750 years. No other astrologers in the known history of our planet have ever deviated from using the stars' actual positions.

How could such a huge mistake have been made and why does it matter? Of course, that was what I asked in my own conversion from Western to Vedic astrology. The answer is it changes all or most of the signs in a horoscope. As a beginning Tropical astrologer, I used to hear astronomers complain: "You astrologers aren't even using correct calculations." Of course, if you think astrology is just entertainment or some frivolous chatter about your ego or a completely subjective opinion from a fortune-teller or psychic, then what does it matter? However, what if the actual position of the stars and planets is critical to understanding their effect? What if astrology is a science based on the stars, which correlates to provable physical events and phenomena? A partial answer would be that the multi-billion dollar Western astrology industry is misinforming millions of people through a huge historical mistake. It would also mean you are probably not the sign you think you are!

The First Beginning

The first beginning is intelligent,
A conscious choice,
An ancient voice,
Eternally wise and joyful, sentient.
Emptiness is unlimited possibility,
Not a goal
Or an empty hole,
In which to spend a useless eternity.
Coming and going is but a gate,
The womb of Tao,
An endless now,
Fullness formed in space, pretending to vacate.
The non-dual context, it
Is seamless being,
Sightless seeing,
An undivided whole we intuit.
That whole reflects as one
Great light,
Destroyer of night,
Never rising or setting, glorious Sun.
The Shiva is a shaft of light,
Ever erect,
Shining direct,
Into the Mother matrix, Kali night.
Stars shine; planets find their course,
Contradiction,
With direction,
Great orgasm from their intercourse.
This pair reflect transcendence,
Time and Space,
Their mad embrace,
The clue is they are two in endless dance.
Before duality, two forms shine,
United and apart,
Of one heart
But each unique and totally Divine.

Jeffrey Armstrong

Chapter Four

You're Probably Not the Sign You Think

It is worth repeating that although I am pointing out a mistake which has entered into Western or Tropical astrology, I do so with respect for anyone who is pursuing the study of our relationship with the Cosmos. If you study history, you will see how easy it is for knowledge to become buried or repressed. Just as we struggle to remember our purpose and vision amidst so many competing forces in our daily life, great wisdom can get lost in the transformative pressures of time. In this discussion of astrology, what is at stake is our link with the stars. *Astrology* literally means *astro* or *star* and *logos* or *logic*. In Sanskrit, it is called *Jyotisha* or *the science of how light regulates life in the realm of matter*. It is also known as *Kala Shastra* or *the science of how time unfolds cause and effect*.

Just as we have a sacred and purposeful relationship with the Earth, we also have a relationship with the stars that is important, sacred and essential to our well-being. In recent times, with the rush to acquire modern scientific knowledge, the importance of these sacred relationships has been neglected for the sake of gaining strictly material knowledge. Now and forever new scientific knowledge needs to be integrated into a personal and meaningful relationship with God, the Cosmos and the Earth.

Although Vedic astrology and Tropical astrology disagree, it is a scientific discussion with importance for everyone. Disagreeing with respect is the basis of our search for truth. Nevertheless, it is important that in our search for truth, complete honesty is partnered with constant love.

Speaking of love, imagine that you were madly in love with someone and had just made love. If you then said to your beloved, "What did you just experience during our lovemaking?" and if they replied with a scientific analysis, "My temperature rose to 99°, my skin became flushed, my blood pressure was 140 over 80 and my pulse became quite rapid"—would that report really explain what you had experienced? Are the facts more important than the emotional and mystical experience of immense love and devotion? On the other hand, if your lover was so ignorant of the physical that they were incompetent to touch you pleasurably, that would also be a problem. Similarly, we have developed an imbalance in our relationship with Nature. There are far too many people who are trampling across the world measuring, tagging and marking everything in sight at the expense of love, aesthetics, spiritual values and quality of life. True science is more than just facts.

If you will, think of astrology as concerned with the balance between two extremes. Any mystical or religious experience can be valid because it is true for you in the depths of your heart. There is no use in arguing or using facts to prove or disprove its reality. It is a special kind of perception, relationship and knowing that does not rest upon external facts relating to matter. On the other hand, at its best, modern science is only concerned with provable facts pertaining to the laws of matter. These two experiences do not need to be in competition, although too often they have been.

The Bridge from Within to Without

Vedic astrology is the bridge between the two realms of experience, internal and external. It uses astronomy to have an accurate picture of the heavens at the moment of birth and then uses that map to discuss the relationship of the individual to the Cosmos, the Earth and the unfoldment of Divine justice. You could say that the astrologer is first a scientist erecting a correct image of a physical event, the stars and planets positions at the time of birth. Then using that image as a tool, the astrologer is an artist, endeavoring to see pre-existing patterns of destiny which are connected to the unfoldment of an individual's destiny. This is where the strictly scientific-minded person becomes frustrated. They are not comfortable making the shift from mere observation of fact to correlations of karmic significance. However, to the Vedic astrologer, the universe is alive, conscious and fully capable of communicating both emotion and meaning.

Unfortunately, Tropical astrologers have drifted away from using the actual positions of the stars by over $23\frac{1}{2}^{\circ}$. That is the next subject for discussion. This inaccuracy does not invalidate their intuitive and emotional relationship to the Cosmos. Nor does it invalidate the gifts of compassion and insight they share with their clients. Nonetheless, both methods of calculation cannot be correct when determining what sign you are.

Sign originally meant and still means a *group of stars*. To deviate from that usage requires a profound justification and explanation. It is after all the science of astrology, so it is best to use the actual positions of the stars as all ancient astrologers intended. If someone discovers a new method of analysis, which is quite possible, then they should be careful to label it differently so no confusion arises between the two methods. I suggest that Western astrology create twelve new names for the seasonal approach and use the current twelve signs of the zodiac as they were originally intended, as names of groups of stars. There are not two zodiacs, as is often said.

47

As for astronomers, they are like the lover who has loads of information about the physical symptoms of love but are missing the emotions and the actual point of the lovemaking. If they gave up their fear of the emotional and spiritual implications of their work, they could discover new ways of knowing, of exploring the correlation between astronomical observation and changes in the individual and world experience. Knowledge and experience are mysteriously connected, as any accomplished lover knows. The real challenge would be to explore the connections between their extensive database of astronomical knowledge to find correlations with the subtleties of human behavior, patterns of weather, epidemics, cultural changes and so on.

A Mistranslation from the Greek

This brings us to how astrology came into Western culture through Arabic and Latin mistranslations of Greek culture and knowledge. How did the error of deviating from the stars originate? Recognition of this error has only taken place during the last 40 years, especially within the last 25 years, due to waves of knowledge coming to the West from India.

Piecing this part of the story together was part of my thirty-year journey. During this time, many Westerners initiated into Vedic understanding have also been pursuing these connections. This is resulting in a renaissance of Vedic arts that includes many forms of yoga, Ayurvedic medicine, martial arts, Vastu Shastra, which is similar to Feng Shui, and of course Vedic astrology. These arts and the corpus of Vedic literature arose before the Greek period of history. Most of us were taught in school that culture, as we know it, started with the Greeks. There is some truth to that view but in recent years we have gained a great deal of previously lost knowledge concerning which of the older civilizations contributed to the development of even Greek culture and philosophy.

From 500 BCE to 300 BCE, Greek culture was in a tremendous state of growth. It was a melting pot of influences from Egypt, India, Babylon, Africa, China, and many others. Socrates lived and taught his famous student Plato, who in turn was teacher to the great Aristotle, who in turn was to teach Alexander the Great. Alexander conquered Babylon in 331 BCE and brought many books on ancient astronomy and astrology from there to Greece. He built the city of Alexandria, which became a major center of learning. He even went as far as Northern India and made significant connections with Indian culture.

There were many talented Greek astronomers during this period. One, named, Erasthones was the head librarian at Alexandria. He measured the size of Earth and was accurate within 400 miles. Another, named Aristarchus, worked out a correct map of the solar system and proved that the Sun—not Earth— was at its center. This shows just how easily such knowledge can be lost. Many great thinkers who followed him still thought Earth was the center of the solar system until the time of Copernicus.

Another Greek astronomer, Hipparchus, using Babylonian and Indian astronomical information, was able to calculate Earth's wobble and thus figure the precession of the equinoxes with some degree of accuracy. He lived from 130 to 60 BCE. This critical knowledge of Earth's wobble would also be forgotten in the chaos of history, resulting ultimately in the error that was passed on to Tropical astrology. Another example of the tendency for great knowledge to get lost in history took place in 47 BCE, when the Roman emperor Julius Caesar was storming the city of Alexandria. He conquered the city but in the process burned the great library to the ground, causing the loss of tremendous knowledge.

The point of all this is to show how an important astronomical and astrological truth could get lost or mixed up in the course of history. The last important Greek astronomer and astrologer who played a part in creating the circumstances of this mistake was Claudius Ptolemy, who lived in Alexandria in 150 AD. He was the last and most influential of the Greek astronomers. He was a great astronomer and wrote a book called *The Almagast*. In fact, his astronomical opinions prevailed in European thought until the 15th century when Copernicus finally proved that the Sun is the center of the solar system. Ptolemy was also an astrologer. He wrote a four-volume book on astrology called *Tetrabiblos*.

The First Day of Spring Is Not Aries

Now it happened that during the time of Ptolemy the vernal equinox, or first day of spring, was still taking place in Aries. His book, written in Greek, states that the first day of spring occurs in the sign of Aries, which at that time was true. Ptolemy probably had no idea that his book would come forward in history as the Western astrological textbook. After his death and the fall of the Roman Empire, European culture remained very stagnant in a time usually called the Dark Ages. Starting in the 7th century, another religion arose and expanded a great empire. Founded by Mohammed, Islam spread and developed a very sophisticated and intellectual culture.

By the 9th century, Baghdad was the new cultural center of the time. Arabic scholars translated many Latin and Greek classics into Arabic. Among these were the *Almagast* and *Tetrabiblos* of Ptolemy. After being translated into Arabic, they eventually were translated into Latin and also English by Western scholars. But the translators were not astrologers or astronomers with sufficient understanding to catch the error. When they translated Ptolemy's astrological classic into English, they translated "On the Vernal Equinox the Sun is in Aries." Neither they nor the astrologers of that time had enough astronomical knowledge to understand that the vernal equinox had moved to Pisces.

By the time *Tetrabiblos* was translated, the first day of spring had been occurring in the star group Pisces for hundreds of years. At that time, no one in Europe understood astronomy or astrology well enough to catch the error. This became the biggest blunder in the history of astrology. Before that time, all astrologers in all cultures, including the Greek, had used the stars' actual positions when creating a horoscope. To further compound this confusion, since the first month or March had coincided with the star group Aries during the Greek time, they named the months of the year Aries, Taurus, Gemini and so on. This is the core of the great confusion. Aries is not a month or time of year, it is a group of stars, a constellation.

To understand this better, imagine two great apparent wheels in space around the Earth. The outermost wheel is a circle of the 12 signs of the zodiac from Aries to Pisces. This is the 360° circle of the fixed stars as they appear 8° either side of the ecliptic. That wheel appears to move very slowly due to the Earth's wobble, at the rate of one revolution in 25,920 years. The other wheel is the cycle of the year as Earth travels once around the Sun. This seasonal wheel is the ecliptic, Earth's path around the Sun.

Think of the big wheel of the constellations as a star cycle and the Earth year as a seasonal cycle. Those two wheels are not the same. It was only a coincidence of history that the Greeks called the first month of the year Aries at a time when the two coincided. Aries is actually a group of stars in the star wheel. That Aries group coincides with spring in the season wheel for only 2,160 years out of every 25,920. Once that time is past, it is no longer correct to say that on March 21st the Sun is in Aries. This year on March 21st the Sun is in Pisces, no matter where on Earth you are and it has nothing to do with any seasonal or geographical considerations.

You Are Not the Sign You Think

In the future, Sun in Aries will occur at Christmas, during winter in the northern latitudes; this will be summer in Australia down south. It is not the seasons that determine your chart; it is the planets' *exact position* in the circle of stars. You are not the sign you think you are and a Vedic astrologer can give you the correct star chart. That sidereal chart is a more accurate tool for explaining your path of destiny and the nature of your body/mind complex of energies. Why this is true is the next step in the unfoldment of the mystery of life that I discovered on my journey of enlightenment.

One of the first Western thinkers to understand the necessity and authenticity of sidereal calculations was Cyril Fagan. He discovered the same truth through studying ancient Egyptian astrological remains. Remember that the important point here is not just a validation of Vedic teachings. If all cultures of old, including the Greek, had continued until today, they would each have a version of sidereal astrology, using essentially the same star-based calculations. Vedic astrology just happens to be the major remaining representative of those older cultures. What Fagan discovered can be found in his excellent book, *Astrological Origins*. It is an intriguing and conclusive analysis, revealing that the Egyptians were astronomer/astrologers at a high level of understanding and that they used that knowledge in the construction of the pyramids and in their daily lives.

From where I stood twenty-seven years ago, I made the leap across a cultural chasm to embrace an older and even more accurate version of astrology. What shocked even me at that time was how much ancient knowledge had been lost and how highly developed it was before it was lost. It seems inconceivable that hard won and precious knowledge would simply be buried and disregarded by following generations. Perhaps some perverse and fickle quality in us demands that we destroy the old and start fresh without regard for the great loss of what has been gained. I call it *fickle-cell anemia*.

Like an unknowing pilgrim on what I thought was a simple journey, I had begun a trek into Himalayan mountains of human understanding. Just as modern science has traveled light years beyond the technology of the past, it happens that the Vedas contain a sophistication of spiritual understanding that is far beyond any other recorded spiritual understanding. In addition, that spiritual knowing is wedded to a material science of immense importance to our survival which must be revived in order to balance the dangers of modern technologies.

What if Vedic astrology is part of a now forgotten revelation that explains the very cause and effect mechanism that underlies human existence? What if it is the remnant of a once great scientific community who understood the causal relationships between the Cosmos, the Earth and the energies and processes that make it function? What if the ancients discovered the *unified field theory* and we lost it? Would it make a difference in your life if you could understand how your day-to-day life is related to and dependent upon the cause and effect principles that animate all life? In my search, I was led next to the ancient material science and cosmology of the Vedas.

The Process of Awakening

Here is the process of awakening,
We are all sleeping in matter.
The first illusion is the smell of earth.
Location is misidentification.
We are real but not solid.
The next veil is the taste of water.
Liquid binds us with sensation.
Feelings cloud our true emotions.
The third layer is fire,
Forms we see, a receding horizon.
The eternal flame does not burn.
The subtle touch of air surrounds us.
Our sensitive skin is an antenna.
Breath is how we stay here.
The silence of space is the veil pass not.
Which by not being binds us
With vibrations in our ears.
Thinking, feeling and willing, our mind
Reflects in us what we are not,
The mirror we cannot resist.
Intellect, the dual state,
Proves what we investigate
With logic rooted in duality.
The last veil is invisible matter
Which we embrace with desire.
Shed it like a serpent skin.
Naked now, the soul in darkness
Pretends that nothing is all,
Night of the soul, nirvana.
Next the ocean of light appears
In which identity is the current,
Keep swimming and don't merge.
Now, all that remains is love,
Which is who we really are,
Each one an eternal star.
And back on Earth, now awake,
The only sign is endless joy
No sorrow can ever take away.

Jeffrey Armstrong

Chapter Five

Five Elements Are Easier Than 106

The next step in understanding Indian star-based astrology requires a description of what science is so that we can discuss the scientific basis of astrology. This will also lead us into a discussion of Ayurvedic medicine, the ancient medical science of India with its cousin Traditional Chinese Medicine (TCM), which includes acupuncture. Perhaps you have heard the famous story from India about the nine blind men trying to describe an elephant. One touched a leg and said the elephant was like a tree or pillar. Another touched the trunk and described the elephant as like a snake. A third touched the elephant's side and described it as like a wall. A fourth touched the tail and described the elephant as being like a broom. All nine had a different experience of the elephant.

This is the way it is for us when we study the universe. One factor is the limitation of our senses (like the blindness) and the other is our state of mind (our preconceptions). For example, the light we see with our eyes is only the light in the visible spectrum from violet (with a wavelength of 390–430 mus) to red (at 650–800 mus). In between those two extremes are indigo, blue, green, yellow and orange. Everything outside that rainbow of visible color is unseen to our unaided eyes; we are blind to it. Even within the range of the visible our eyes fool us. For example, objects at a distance appear small, even though they are not.

From this, you might say that any science is limited in some way by its measuring equipment. Because our senses are connected to the mind and the mind can project images or beliefs onto our perceptions, we often see what we want to see or expect to see. Magicians performing slight of hand are able to create amazing illusions by tricking our mind into a certain expectation. Part of the illusion is that our mind expects to see a certain outcome. In the case of the blind men, flat meant wall, round and tall meant pillar and so on. Like them, we often see what our mind says we are seeing rather than what is before us. This is where thinkers found themselves at the beginning of the modern scientific revolution. They observed that most people's beliefs about matter were either incorrect or were a reflection of a particular religious or philosophical view, rather than something that could be proven.

The famous story of Galileo and his experiment with falling objects illustrates this well. Aristotle had previously stated that two objects of different weight would fall at correspondingly different rates. That view had been accepted on faith by scholars of the time. Galileo experimented by dropping two objects of dissimilar weight from the Leaning Tower of Pisa and discovered that they both fell at the same speed. He proved Aristotle wrong. Many of his contemporaries did not appreciate an unknown thinker trying to prove the great Aristotle, who was an accepted authority, wrong. Thus, their belief in Aristotle was a state of mind, which blocked their senses from really seeing the elephant. Naturally this led the growing scientific movement to the realization that religion was often blocking perception with belief. One of the most dramatic examples of this conflict was the issue of whether the Earth or the Sun is the center of the universe.

Like Aristotle, Ptolemy was a Greek thinker whose influence was immense and, by the 15th century in Europe, his views on astronomy were still being accepted on blind faith. It was his view that the Earth is the center of the universe and that the Sun revolves around the Earth. He believed this despite the fact that Greek and Indian thinkers before him had demonstrated that the Earth is round and that the Sun is the center of the solar system.

Religious Influence on Astrology

Unfortunately, the Catholic Church had adopted Ptolemy and Aristotle as authorities. They then tied their own authority to those views. The result was they became terrified the scientific view would undermine belief in God as they were presenting Him. Their unfortunate response was to burn people at the stake. Indeed, the word *heresy*, as it was used then, meant *to form an opinion*. This created a very dangerous climate for thinkers who were simply trying to discover the truths of natural law. At that time, you could be killed for holding a different view of the elephant than the one held by the rest of the blind men. The assumption in all this was that there is only one "right" answer to any question and that you should be killed for speaking the "wrong" answer. The unfortunate effects of this war over truth are still with us today.

Eventually, as science grew in strength and momentum, the war extended to Darwin's theories and the debate over creationism vs. evolutionism. As the age of discovery proceeded, various cultures like India, China and the rest were invaded by Judeo/Christian cultures. By then, the war between religion and science was in full swing. Christians came into these cultures assuming that Christianity was the only truth and scientists went in assuming that all older cultures were ignorant, unscientific and primitive. Neither one was inclined to take a close look at the wisdom and science which had been accumulated over tens of thousands of years of human experience in these ancient cultures.

It has taken a few more generations for the smoke to settle in this war of viewpoints. As science has matured through the relativistic views of Einstein and the quantum revolutions in thinking, it is beginning to lose that hard edge which claimed there was only one "right" view. While we are still in danger of having various forms of technology forced upon us by vested economic interests, many people are now embracing alternative models of healing and living. Those models do not negate the prevailing scientific view; they are actually a different but parallel kind of scientific understanding.

As for religion, we are all watching anxiously to see if people can learn to hold strong beliefs without going to war. By now, the irony of killing in the name of Jesus, Allah, Jehovah, Buddha or Krishna (the embodiments of universal love, wisdom, and compassion) should not be lost on anyone. If the age of information means anything, it must be an opportunity to evolve to a higher level of perfection by absorbing the best from all cultures instead of blindly adhering to any one.

This is a prelude to introducing another scientific method that was developed in the East at least ten thousand years ago. It is not primitive; it is very sophisticated. It is not in competition with the modern scientific viewpoint and it is not merely a religious belief, though at a certain point it is integrated into a metaphysical viewpoint. A good word for describing the various models of perception used by science and religion is that they are *paradigms*. Each method is both a power and a limitation. Take the example of mathematics. The decimal system of math, 1–10 including zero, is very useful for everyday math. Perhaps ten is good for us since we have ten fingers but 1–10 was not as useful when it came to creating computers. Computers work based on a binary system of math, which expresses all numbers as strings of ones and zeros.

I don't know anyone who uses binary math to balance their checkbook. For everyday use, binary math is not useful, yet without it there would be no computers. So which view is right, binary or decimal? Shall we burn one at the stake and keep the other or could we be like the blind men looking at the elephant? In a way, the nine men were all right and all wrong at the same time. This is an Eastern view. Everyone's view of truth is to be respected; each has some truth. The territory of science is the provable. The territory of religion is the unprovable, yet essential to understand the purpose of life. I propose that Vedic astrology is the bridge between them, with one foot in the provable and one in the metaphysical. For the moment, let's look at the scientific paradigm on which Vedic astrology and Ayurvedic medicine both rest.

The Basic Building Materials

As a point of comparison, let's start out with something everyone understands from modern science. What we call matter is actually made up of invisible component parts called *atoms*. Each atom has a particular atomic structure, which identifies it as an atom of a particular element. There are about 106 elements in the current periodic table of elements. If you were to analyze any material object with sensitive equipment, you could measure the relative amounts of each element that are present. This would constitute one method of describing the thing. It has this much carbon, this much zinc, this much hydrogen, this much oxygen and so on.

I have never personally seen an atom but I am reasonably certain that something like these elements does exist in Nature. It is not immediately obvious just by looking that the atomic elements are present. In fact, at one time, you would have been thought insane or heretical to believe in the existence of invisible atoms. But now, we have learned to see the elephant within the context of the 106 elements and, for some purposes, it is extremely useful. The secret of this kind of paradigm is that everything we see can be reduced to some combination of these elements as one aspect of its underlying nature.

Thousands of years ago, our early ancestors also created a unique scientific paradigm. They looked at the world around them and asked the same question: "What are the basic elements that make up the content of what I see, touch, feel, taste, smell and hear in the world around me?" The answer formed the basis of another scientific paradigm, which also has a periodic table of elements. The elements of this model are the solid (earth), the liquid (water), the burning (fire), the gaseous (air) and the encompassing (space). These are the five fundamental elements of our perception. There is nothing within our physical experience which is beyond or outside these five categories. More to the point, everything we experience through our senses is some discernable mixture of earth, water, fire, air and space— that is a scientific fact! Once you have adjusted to seeing the universe through this simpler model, the next step is to realize that just as your body can be described by some combination of the 106 periodic elements, it can also be described as some combination of the five elements.

This five-element model of the universe was adopted from India by the ancient Greek doctors and is still used by Ayurvedic and Chinese medical practitioners. The advantage of five-element science is that the qualities of the five elements can be perceived by our unaided senses. Take fire or water for example. We know that in its natural state water is liquid, absorbent and cool. Fire is hot, radiant, burning, and gives off energy and light. The acid with which we digest food is actually a fire which cooks the food we eat in the pot of our stomach. At any moment, our body is either hot or cold, and on a day-to-day basis, hot and cold are very important to our well-being. If we become cold, we go sit in the Sun or near a fire or make a cup of hot tea.

Following the logic that everything in the world is simply made of some combination of the five elements, it follows that some things will be of more fire, of more water, of more earth, of more air or of more space—exactly in the way some things have more iron, zinc, copper, carbon or more sulfur. The principle is the same, but one uses 106 invisible elements and the other uses the five elements we see with our unaided senses. If you extend this line of thinking, everything in Nature has more or less of one or another of the five elements.

Let's use fire as an example and look for things with fire in them. The hot foods like ginger root, cayenne and black pepper are heating. They have more fire in them. If you eat these foods, you will then have more fire in you. This may seem simple but is in fact very powerful on a day-to-day basis if you are trying to remain balanced. The basis of our perception of the five elements is that certain qualities can be examined with our unaided senses. Rough, smooth, dry, wet, hot, cold, oily, light, heavy— each of these is perceptible and each is associated with one of the five elements. There are many books available these days that explain Ayurvedic foods and diet in further detail.

Ten Pairs of Material Qualities

Heavy	Light
Cold	Hot
Unctuous	Rough
Dull	Sharp
Stable	Mobile
Soft	Hard
Slimy	Dry
Smooth	Coarse
Minute	Gross
Solid	Liquid

The Point and Click User Interface

To make this easier to understand, let's compare Nature to a computer. Computers are made in layers. The layer closest to the machine only responds to varying states of electricity which cause gates to open and close. That level is run by binary mathematics which communicates with strings of ones and zeroes. Most people would not use computers if they needed to work at that level of complexity. On top of that level is another layer and another on top of that until eventually there is the operating system of the computer. In the case of PC DOS, even that layer is not very friendly to most humans, so Windows was developed. Windows is a user interface which was designed to be more intuitive and easier for the average person to figure out and manage. It is a point and click level of use of the otherwise complicated computer. When the user in Windows gives a command, it is eventually translated into the binary language which causes its execution at the machine level.

Similarly, whatever is true at the level of the 106 elements is also true at the level of the five elements. Both are the same reality seen in a simple or complex way. The five-element science is the "Windows" point and click user interface to the world of matter, which makes us up and surrounds us. Both are equally scientific; one is just more complex. Ancient scientists used this five-element scientific model to categorize everything in Nature according to its elemental mixture. Everything is made of some precise proportion of the five and will therefore change whatever it is added to in a predictable way. The qualities of the five elements are the basis of a powerful science that interfaces our bodily senses with the objects and energies in Nature.

Hear My Voice

Amid the crushing noise of this world,
The crashing, banging and strife,
In this maelstrom where we were hurled,
Beneath the roar of life,
Gentle voices are whispering,
A hushed and invisible throng,
Sings in the heart of everything,
If we listen to hear their song.
I am space; my song is a lark,
Womb of vibrations above,
Hear my voice in the heart of the dark,
The first vibration of love.
I am air; my song is wind,
Mover of life in the sky,
Touching the surface, I take you within,
To a place where you never die.
I am Fire, my song is light,
The truth is all I know,
Live with honor, feel my might,
Hear my voice and you'll know.
I am water; my song is of love,
I flow within your veins,
Pregnant clouds floating above,
Hear my voice when it rains.
I am earth; my song is of trust,
I live beneath your feet,
Patiently holding your life on my crust,
Hear my sound in your heartbeat.

Jeffrey Armstrong

Chapter Six

Making Friends with the Five Elements

Space, the Invisible Beginning

Once upon a time an academic scientist went to visit a Zen Master, famous for being very wise. After greeting the scholar, the master offered him tea. As they sat together, the monk began to pour the tea into the scholar's cup. He poured until the tea overflowed onto the saucer, then the table and finally onto the floor.

When the scholar could not stand it any more, he blurted out: "Stop, stop, can't you see the cup is full?" To which the Zen Master replied: "Yes, I can, and until your mind is empty, you will not hear what I have to say."

It is like that as we begin to discuss the element of space. If you remember your 6th grade science class, the teacher said something about the primitive Greeks, who: "Before there were real scientists, used to believe the world was made of only five elements. They believed the first of those five elements was space. Of course scientists have now proven that space is not an element since it has no qualities." Does this mean that space doesn't exist? If not, then what did the Ancients mean by saying that space is the first element? As it turns out, the science of fifty years ago was not able to understand what is now better understood. Space is not empty; it is full of potential. The way the ancients saw this was that *space is that from which everything is emerging*. Space is an empty full, which accommodates life. It is a type of cosmic womb energy, out of which and within which all life exists. Similarly, on a day-to-day basis space makes room for life. An empty room is space in which to live. A pause in a conversation is space in which to reply. Space is the Great Mother of life.

This is also one of the secrets taught in martial arts. The masters observed that the images we hold in our mind prevent us from directly perceiving the reality in front of us. They told their students to empty their minds so they could really see what was in front of them. The same is true from a psychological perspective. If the mind is full of thoughts and memories, especially if they are painful, it becomes distressed and begins to break down. Treatments like electrical and chemical shock therapy were developed to erase short-term memory, thus creating some space. That's the hard way. Many meditative techniques do something similar but more gently. Often the old self must die symbolically, in order to create room or space for the development of a new self, the space within which to manifest new creation.

If you look closely at Chinese paintings, especially Taoist art, you will notice large areas of empty space. There are some natural rock formations, flowing water, a little vegetation and a small and humble presence of something human. Obviously a culture based on space would be less concerned with material possessions. With the five elements as a reference, it becomes clear every culture has intentionally or intuitively "worshipped" one or more of the elements and made it prominent in their art and culture.

Another place where space has manifest in the arts is science fiction. As our planet has become better known and less mysterious—once we climbed the mountains, fenced the land, harnessed fire, flew through the air and crossed over and under the water—the only remaining element of mystery to us is space. Films like *Star Trek* say it clearly: "Space, the final frontier." And as we imagine what could be out there, the sky's the limit.

But space travel is nothing new. It has been the regular practice of yogis and great thinkers throughout time. The only difference now is that we have made expensive and cumbersome ships, which can only carry a few people. Space and what is beyond space is indeed the "final frontier"!

Day to day we also notice when someone is "spaced out." We will also tell someone if they need to "give us some space." What may not be obvious to us is that the person who is spaced out actually has more of the element space in their constitution. Or they may have eaten food or taken a drug which induced a spacey condition. As we will see later, this forms the basis of dietary and herbal therapeutic principles in both Ayurvedic and Chinese medicine. Similarly, the person who is not giving you space is no doubt suffering from an imbalance of that element, causing a lack of regard for other's space.

The element space has only one perceivable characteristic: it is able to conduct energy. Otherwise it cannot be touched, seen, tasted or smelled. Space is filled with what we have come to know as cosmic rays. At either end of the visible light spectrum there are vibrations or frequencies of energy. If we could see those frequencies with our eyes or hear them with our ears, space would appear full rather than empty. It is now provable that our physical and mental being is constantly being tuned or vibrated by those unseen cosmic energies. We are literally reverberating with the music of the heavens.

ELEMENT: Space

SANSKRIT NAME: Akasha

KEY WORDS: Motionless, Accommodating, Expansive, Enveloping, Detached, Open, Receptive, Cavity, Abyss, Orifice, Gap, Still, Static, Quiet, Inert, Torpor, Endless, Languid, Stable, Stagnant, Rest, Commodious, Extensive, Voluminous, Capacious, Comprehensive.

ACTION: Be Open.
RULE: Space rules by encompassing.
SYMBOLIC FORM: Black Egg.

Wind, the All-Pervasive Harmonizer

The second element to manifest is air or wind. Within the emptiness of space, a gaseous condition has manifest. Those bubbles of air have formed pockets, which are denser than space. They cannot be seen but they can be felt. And since the air element is constantly in motion, we call it wind. As the subtlest of the four gross elements, it pervades everything. It also precedes everything, which is to say that everything that exists is a condensation from a previous gaseous state. Everything is connected by wind. At birth, our first contact with life is to breathe, that is, to take in life. From that time until death, we are fed life through breath. By nature the wind is cold, restless, subtle and dry.

The normal rate of breathing is about 15 breaths per minute or 900 per hour, which is 21,600 per day. In a year that would be 7,884,000 breaths, and if one lived a hundred years.... 700,884,000 puffs of air. This automatic process of inhaling life energy is so subtle and automatic that most of us do not even pay attention to its importance. In everyday speech, when we are enlivened and eager to live, we call it inspiration. Spirit—living breath—has entered our being, a metaphor which can be found in most traditional creation stories.

In the Old Testament of the Bible, God blows the breath of life into his newly created humans. In yogic practice, this *air of life* is called *prana*; the *art of controlling the body/mind complex by regulating the life air* is called *pranayama*. We shall discuss this further in a later chapter, but for now it is important to understand that the element wind is related to the nervous system and brain, as well as all forms of communication. It is not only the primal source of energy but also the balance of the more dense elements which follow.

The Vedas of India have an interesting variation on this theme. It is said that God created the entire universe as a great body. Each part of that body was also personified as an Angel, or Deva as they are called. So it was that the eyes, ears, limbs and other body parts were all represented by a different personality. Each Deva has a female counterpart called a Devi and each pair of Devas is said to control one aspect of the universe, such as water or fire or the eyes and legs and so on. One day, all the parts of this universal form got together to decide whose role was the most important. To decide this, each Deva and Devi would leave the body and stay away for some time. Upon their return they would ask: "How did you live without us?" When the eyes left and returned the rest of the Devas said: "We lived as a blind man, we could not see." And so it went with all the Devas until finally Vayu, the Deva of Wind, withdrew from the body. Immediately the body died and fell to the ground. When the god of wind returned, they all agreed that his role as the life air was the most important.

ELEMENT: Air or Wind

SANSKRIT NAME: Vayu

KEY WORDS: Flexible, Alert, Dynamic, Subtle, Mobile, Moving, Kinetic, Circulating, Active, Flux, Motility, Motion, Vital, Energetic, Vigorous, Driving, Acute, Sharp, Astir, Vibrant, Animate, Essential, Atmospheric, Thin,

Insubstantial, Tenuous, Immaterial, Delicate, Rough, Oscillating.

ACTION: Be Subtle.
RULE: Wind rules with movement.
SYMBOLIC FORM: Light Blue Circle.

Fire, the Great Transformer

The next in order of descending manifestation of these great elements, or *mahabhutas* as they are called in Sanskrit, is fire. Due to friction within the wind, fire is generated. Heat, light, electricity and form are related to this element. Fire is the great transformative agent in the universe; it is literally cooking everything. Cooking means changing the form and structure. At the heart of matter is the pivotal action of fire. The hearth where it burns in our house is etymologically related to the heart. Everything that lives seeks and uses the light and heat of the Sun to conduct the transformations that make life possible.

Photosynthesis, the basic transformation of sunlight into usable energy, is the result of the elements meeting on Earth creating what we call food. In fact, digestion is also a cooking of food. All energetic transformations are a process of reshaping conducted by fire. Fire is energetic and penetrating. This is the point at which color becomes manifest. This element is visible, and its light reveals the nature of everything it touches. Just as plants always grow toward the light of the Sun, what we call history is the story of how cultures have grown through the use of fire. The recent explosion of physical transformation on our planet and the attendant dangers are clear evidence of the power of fire.

The study of physical science is primarily the study of energies related to fire. That is why the two great laws that underlie physics are the two laws of thermodynamics, which is to say the laws of the action of fire. They are: "Matter is neither created or destroyed, it is merely transformed" and "All matter is going from a higher state of energy to a lower and in the process giving off heat and waste." The latter is known as the law of entropy. In simple terms it means that wherever a fire is burning, fuel will be consumed, producing some energy and some waste. This is also why realizations on the nature of the universe, like Einstein's revelations regarding relativity, are stated in terms of the speed of light. Astronomy, similarly, is the study of light over distance and time, the larger metabolic processes of the universal body. These are all studies of the transformative influence of fire.

On a personal level, each of us uses fire every day for many obvious and many subtle life processes. Mental digestion of ideas is a fire process just as much as the digestion of food. Fire manifests the world of color and reserves the color red as its own. To perceive the presence of fire, look around for those things that are red. Look to see what is digesting, eating, transforming, heating and revealing the world. Fire is always the staunch enemy of darkness and inertia. Light drives away dark but dark never drives away light. The excessive use of fire is dangerous. In fact, fire is always dangerous and burns anyone who abuses it, as many with too much firepower are inclined to do.

Another quality of fire is hunger. Fire will burn an unlimited amount of fuel. There is no limit except that imposed by wind, which must be present, and fuel, which is some form of earth. As anyone knows, water puts out fire. Fire heats up water. This is the steam engine that runs the universe.

ELEMENT: Fire

SANSKRIT NAME: Agni

KEY WORDS: Focused, Clear, Intense, Energetic, Assimilative, Digesting, Consuming, Blazing, Glowing, Incendiary, Burning, Illuminating, Igneous, Light,

Empyrean, Ignescent, Concentrated, Forceful, Hot, Vehement, Excited, Combustible, Eating.

ACTION: Be Intense.
RULE: Fire rules with intensity.
SYMBOLIC FORM: Red Triangle.

Water, the Universal Solvent

The next transformation of the one universal energy is caused by the formation of the primal liquid energy—water. Cool and flowing by nature, this energy is that into which everything is dissolved. Women's bodies have approximately 5% more water than men, so this is the feminine force which acts as the womb of life. Just as the amniotic fluid of a mother allows the transmission of nutrients from her body to the embryo, so in life water is the great mother. Space is the womb and water is that which supports and nourishes life. In the Cosmos, the Moon, which controls the tides, is the planetary counterpart of the water element. The menstrual cycle and lunar cycle are interrelated and regulate the flow of this life-giving fluid. In many ways, water is life.

Water is yielding and gentle in action, giving way, assuming the form of its container, seeking the lowest level. The rock is worn away by water one drop at a time, with persistence. Water holds the particles and vibrations of whatever it touches, transporting them from place to place. It is associated with deluge and oblivion, for when water is supreme, everything is dissolved. Form is lost and so we see the central polarity and opposition of the actions of fire and water. Fire, identified with the Sun, is the mover of water, with its great energy. Water is the negation of fire, quenching it just as it does our thirst. Without water, the fire of our being would burn us endlessly. These two elements act as the pistons of a perpetual motion machine called the universe, a machine made of subtle energies. Expanding and contracting, building up and dissolving, they work together with air to form a trinity of active forces that make up our life.

Our bodies are mostly water. Throughout history, great civilizations have arisen on the banks of mighty rivers and disappeared when the waters dried up or changed course. Water is purifying and holy by its very nature: cleanliness is next to Godliness. It is associated with joyfulness, sensuality, emotions and nourishment. Breast milk is also a fluid, so the primal waters of the universe are the life-giving energy. But when the waters become too great and break the boundaries that contain them, all of life is submerged and washed away. At that time, or in the vast oceans, water represents that which is unseen, unconscious and unfathomable.

ELEMENT: Water

SANSKRIT NAME: Jala

KEY WORDS: Fluid, Flowing, Cool, Creative, Emotional, Liquid, Dilutant, Wet, Damp, Vapor, Cloudy, Misty, Douse, Drench, Saturate, Imbue, Dabble, Humidity, Aqueous, Whelm, Soppy, Hydrous, Oozy, Sodden, Dewy, Dank, Muggy, Soggy, Clammy.

ACTION: Be Fluid.
RULE: Water rules with persistence.
SYMBOLIC FORM: Silver Blue Crescent.

Earth, the Platform of Life

The last of the five elements—the one with which we are the most familiar is earth. Earth is the platform on which we are living. It is that which argues most convincingly that reality is tangible. In fact, earth is the rarest of elements in the universe. It is the exception and not the rule. But for us it is Mother Earth, the one at whose breast we are fed, play, work, live and die. We are now at the opposite end of the descent begun at space. The earth element contains all the five qualities: sound, touch, sight, taste and its own smell. Who can forget the smell of a newly plowed field on a spring day? This is earth; the objects of our desire are all made of it.

Earth is solid. It is the basis of everything and allows growth. It provides stability and boundaries. It is rigid and strong. It is the cornucopia, the horn of plenty from which all foods pour forth. Earth is full of life and mysterious in that it is the most dense and impenetrable. Earth is dark and cold until it receives the light of the Sun. Like its neighbor water, it must receive outside energy to produce life. It also contains fire in some inexplicable way— at the heart of earth is fire, the core of Earth is molten rock. Again . . . it is the hearth, the place where we transform life with fire in the midst of water while supported by air and accommodated by space.

Earth is the most solid energy, so much so that it appears to be truly substantial. Yet closer examination reveals that earth is not permanent. It is subject to gradual change and eventual destruction. Those who realize this often renounce the earth element. At the other end of the spectrum, some people are so covered in earth that they are literally buried in it. When acting as a negative force, the earth element is dark, full of inertia and obstacles. It causes lethargy and attachment. At its best the earth element provides the place, the platform on which life takes place. You can't play tennis without a court. Earth is the playing field that both challenges and limits us. It holds fire or water in place and is closely related to wind by being cold and dry by nature. Earth is the most contracted, rigid and condensed form of cosmic energy. It is our home, the place where we rest. Earth holds life in place and is the center around which life revolves.

ELEMENT: Earth

SANSKRIT NAME: Prithivi

KEY WORDS: Stable, Concrete, Solid, Grounded, Terrestrial, Coarse, Crude, Steady, Firm, Stalwart, Material, Hard, Compact, Dense, Tight, Massive, Lumpy, Physical, Substantial, Strong, Stout, Tough, Stiff, Tense, Constant, Stable, Unvarying, Unwavering.

ACTION: Be Solid.
RULE: Earth rules with patience.
SYMBOLIC FORM: Yellow Square.

Character of the Five Elements

ELEMENT	SPACE	AIR	FIRE	WATER	EARTH
PERCEP-TIVE SENSE	Ear	Skin	Eye	Tongue	Nose
ACTIVE SENSE	Mouth	Hands	Feet	Genitals	Anus
SENSORY SENSE	Hearing	Touch	Sight	Taste	Smell
NATURE	Accom-modate	Move	Transform	Dissolve	Stabilize
ACTIVITY	Enclose	Disperse	Cook	Transport	Support
DESIRE	Create	Move	Change	Merge	Endure
FAULT	Detached	Restless	Angry	Lusty	Greedy

How to Use the Five Elements in Your Life

These five elements are deceptively simple. Because modern science has developed an extremely complex and sophisticated view of the same material Nature, they are inclined to disregard this simpler model. The power of the five elements is that they are perceivable by our unaided senses. Everything that surrounds us is made of them. What is amazing is that we can learn to see the proportions of each element present in our food, medicines, climate, belongings, environment, our body and the bodies of those around us.

This is the simplest model of analyzing the physical world that is available to our unaided senses. Therefore it is the ultimate interface between Nature and us. It is always true and always available. Modern scientific models are too complicated and elaborate for everyday use. We cannot see the distinctions of microscopic science, so they only confuse and disempower us in any situation where we must make a choice.

Take food as an example. All food is made of varying amounts of the five elements. If a particular food has more water and earth, it will be cold and heavy like those elements. If you have a heavy body that is inclined to be cold and you eat cold and heavy food during cold and wet weather, can you see the obvious imbalance this would create? If you made a conscious choice about everything in your surroundings, as if you were trying to achieve balance, you would be constantly making decisions about the effect of combinations of the five elements. Your relationship to Nature would become scientific in a new way.

Eventually you will understand the elemental makeup of all the foods, herbs and spices in your life. Just imagine that instead of cooking simply for taste or from emotional impulse, you could eat scientifically the foods compatible with your own elemental needs. Everyone in your family would have their own particular needs according to how their body is working at any time. It just takes a little practice to implement this knowledge as a lifestyle.

The five elements are also used in spiritual practice. Our body is composed of a mixture of the five elements woven into a very subtle fabric. Yet according to the Vedas, that body is not our true and eternal self. It is a vehicle that we create out of matter for our purposes in the material world. One aspect of meditation is the observation of the difference between consciousness and the matter that is its current vehicle. That process is called separating the five great elements.

In other words, from one angle we use the five elements to scientifically build our body. From another angle we observe that our true self is different than matter when it is necessary to leave the physical. When the five-element knowledge is used to build our bodies, it empowers us with the ability to harmonize with the larger forces of Nature that surround us. When we dismantle the five elements by observing our self to be different than them, we achieve the power of detachment from what is not our true self.

In my journey of understanding Vedic astrology, I was led to an understanding of five-element science. The descriptive language of astrology is of the four elements. There are earth signs, water signs, fire signs and air signs. In other words, the horoscope is couched in the same scientific terms as five-element science. After all, the horoscope is attempting to describe a being formed in material Nature, who is made of some combination of the five great energies. What more natural language to use! As you might have guessed, the thinkers who embraced five-element science applied it to the field of medicine. There are many useful divisions of Ayurvedic medicine, which are available to enlighten our lifestyle choices. Hopefully, it will soon be recognized for the true medical science that it is and integrated with other scientific models.

The next piece of our puzzle has to do with how bodies are created out of the five elements and the system of medicine that arose from their understanding. It is another amazing fact of history that an incredibly sophisticated medical system was fully developed in Bharata by 800 BCE. It included plastic surgery, anesthesia, brain surgery, acupuncture points and meridians and full instructions for cataract operations. It also included a complete cataloging of food and herbs according to their effects in terms of the five elements. Let's take a look at the ten body types and Ayurvedic medicine.

Dragon Dreams Phoenix Rises

I live within the unspeakable silence,
By the rules of another science,
Hermetically sealed, the cauldron, I
Am patiently turning with the sky.
A dragon dreams but cannot wake,
The phoenix rises for his sake
And so he bathes her with his tears,
While she sings love songs in his ears.
I fly but never leave the ground,
On a silver ship with wings of sound,
Within a lotus born of earth,
A universe did not take birth
And never coming, never goes,
Yet from this every other grows.
I sit beyond the speed of light,
Which is a veil upon the night.
Hiding planets wrapped in air,
Transverse dimensions, unaware.
I live in orbs of shimmering love,
Where so below is as above.

Jeffrey Armstrong

Chapter Seven

Ten Body Types
of Which Yours Is One

Anyone who studies the Vedas with an open mind is in for a series of shocking revelations. One of the most compelling of those enlightenments is that a sophisticated medical system was developed in ancient times which is still far beyond our current understanding of the healing process. Ayurvedic medicine is definitely not mentioned or credited in modern medical history or world history. Yet it is the source of amazing understandings about how we are produced from Nature and how to work harmoniously with those creative processes.

Between 800 and 500 BCE, Ayurvedic medicine had reached its pinnacle and produced two important books: The *Charaka Samhita* and the *Shushruta Samhita*. The first is a general compendium on medicine, while the second is a detailed manual on surgery. The surgical text includes an extensive description of instruments for surgery including anesthesia, brain surgery, rhinoplasty or plastic surgery to replace body parts and detailed descriptions of procedures for cataract operations.

The *Shushruta Samhita* also gives details of the workings of what it calls the *marma points*, developed and popularized by Traditional Chinese Medicine as acupuncture points. Astounding as it is, this means the ancients had discovered the DC electrical current within our bodies and mapped its relationship to the internal organs of the body and cycles of Nature. There now exist modern acupuncture point locators that measure electrical activity at the skin. They locate the points in the exact positions predicted by the ancients 3,000 or more years ago. Does anyone have an explanation?

With all due respect to our modern medical establishment for their various achievements, their arrogance and refusal to listen to other methods of healing is a blight on modern culture. All too often they are merely pawns in the marketing manipulations of the chemical and pharmaceutical manufacturers who are only interested in controlling, owning and patenting every important natural resource on the planet. This is the real cause of both our forgetfulness of Ayurvedic medicine and a myriad of other similar healing modalities which could be of such healing service. It is time to stop the madness of allowing natural healing substances to be controlled by entrepreneurs with no understanding or care for the importance of natural medical systems.

Both Chinese and Ayurvedic medicine have existed for thousands of years and should be respected by modern science and the FDA. Instead, they remain illegal or undervalued as an extension of the colonial violence that has almost destroyed these ancient gifts. At the basis of the Ayurvedic medical system is the five-element scientific model. One of its greatest understandings is a system of body-typing that informs us of our visible relationship with the formative energies of Nature.

How Our Bodies Are Formed by Nature

Understanding how our bodies are formed by Nature is a crucial piece to understanding the proper purposes of astrology and many other important subtle connections. In my journey of awakening, this was another important revelation. What is true for everything in Nature is also true for our bodies. The complicated way to describe our unique body type is through our genetic code. The simple way to describe that same reality is by observing the mix of the five elements which are present in each body. That is something we can see with our unaided senses if we are trained to do so.

On the way to combining the five elements, a funny thing happens. It appears that Nature likes to do things in threes. The five elements form three distinct groups when they combine to make a body. Space and air blend into a substance called *vata*. Fire, which is called *pitta*, stands by itself, though it always needs air and earth as fuel to burn. Water and earth form a kind of mud or clay, which is called *kapha*. These three are called *doshas*, which means an *imperfect or faulty thing*. Because they are formed of five separate elements that keep separating and are difficult to hold together, the doshas are unstable. Our bodies are an unsteady alliance of the five elements.

Every body has vata, pitta and kapha or space/air (movement and communication), fire (digestion or transformation) and water/earth (cohesion, substance, lubrication). To exist, a body must have all three, but every body has them in varying proportions. If someone is thin, cold, nervous, dry, unsteady and light, they are predominantly vata. If someone is of medium build, hot, intense, muscular, with sharp appetite, acidic, red-faced and aggressive, then they are predominantly pitta. And if someone is heavy, moist, oily, stable, nurturing and solid, they are predominantly kapha.

Perhaps you have heard of a similar description of three body types: ectomorph, mesomorph and endomorph. *Morph* means *body*, *ecto* means *skin*, *meso* means *muscle and bone* and *endo* means *gut* or *lymphatics*. The three types are centered on a predominant natural process. The vata, or ectomorph, is focused on communication and the nervous system, represented externally by the skin. The pitta, or mesomorph, is focused on the bones, muscles and strength. The kapha, or endomorph, is focused upon the gut and lymphatic processes. To apply this to yourself: first decide which one of the three you have been most like throughout your life. Are you slender, nervous, refined, high-strung, a light sleeper and often cold in the extremities? If so, you are a vata. Are you of medium build, muscular, forceful, hot, impatient, with very strong digestion? If so, you are a pitta. Are you heavy, slow, steady, nurturing, sluggish, moist and inactive? If so, you are a kapha. Remember that, at this point, you only get to choose one.

Ecto, Meso, Endo Morphing

The ecto, meso, endo terminology came from the work of a psychologist named William Sheldon, who lived in the 1930's. He took the idea from the four humors of the Greeks, who had inherited their medical system from India 2,500 years ago when the five-element science was at its peak. As children there was a game we used to play called scissors, paper and rock. Have you played it? Paper is the open hand, rock a fist, scissors the extended index and middle fingers. The rules are simple: Paper covers rock, rock breaks scissors and scissors cut paper. At the count of three we each choose. Somebody wins, somebody loses or we draw. Like this game, the three doshas, that are really the five elements, combine and recombine. From the first point of cosmic manifestation, all the way down to Earth, various patterns and combinations of the elements create everything. At each level of the process of manifestation, the combinations vary.

Most people can see their primary body type with a little guided self-examination. In fact, you can usually see that one type is primary, another secondary and the third less visible.

The combination of the three doshas gives rise to ten basic body types:

. vata, vata/pitta, vata/kapha
. pitta, pitta/vata, pitta/kapha
. kapha, kapha/vata, kapha/pitta
. tridoshic, when all three are balanced (rare)

Space is the great distance context that surrounds us. We feel only remotely connected to space, while the earth elements feel like home to us. Thus, the most dynamic elements of our daily experience are three: wind, fire and water. After all, what is the yearly weather cycle if not varying degrees of hot or cold and wet or dry, surrounded and pervaded by moving currents of air. It is not only weather, it is life. Wind, rain, sun and clouds constantly swirl around us playing scissors, paper and rock with our lives. Fire burns, water wets, winds blow; they intertwine to form the fabric of our life. They are the active energies, while space appears static and earth appears immobile.

In this game of life, fire and water are the most opposite and air is the great mediator, the harmonizer, balancing or disturbing, all pervasive and subtle. The day-to-day duality of our lives is fire/water, hot/cold, wet/dry or dark/light. These energies also correspond with the world of colored forms which surround us. In order to see the various combinations of energy better, let us envision each element as a color. Of course everything is made of all five elements in some proportion. The emergence of three forces as the three most dynamic energies is part of a natural tendency to build the physical out of three components in dynamic relation to each other.

Learning to See the Three Doshas

For the moment, let's simplify this and say there are only three types of people: fire, water and air or pitta, kapha and vata. Likewise for food, weather, herbs—anything made of the five elements—will fall into one of these three categories. This is the first step of a universal method of keeping track of the energy we touch in the world around us. Is it hot or cold? Is it wet or dry? Air is dry and cold by nature. Fire is hot and dry by nature. Water is wet and cold by nature but can become hot up to a point. If you practice this simple exercise, you will begin to see these three things everywhere. Reduce all your perceptions to these three categories until you see them everywhere. Once you are able to see the five elements through their qualities, it will be easy to see the three doshas that are combinations of the elements. After establishing the primary dosha, the secondary is usually obvious. With the primary and secondary understood, you are now in possession of a permanent code, like the genetic code, that will be the physical basis of a given body throughout its existence.

This is truly the unconscious mind. People are acting according to their elemental nature at every moment but are unconscious of the interconnectedness of all life through the elemental relations. Outside our bodies, the five elements exist as raw elements. When they come together to create a human, plant or animal body, they transform into three specialized bodily substances. Those three transmit and embody the energy of space, wind, fire, water and earth. That constitution, like our genetic material, is constant. If you are born a fire type, you will die a fire type; it is immutable. Your body type can be modified but not changed. At first, it is hard to grasp the full magnitude of the ten body types. We are accustomed to viewing ourselves and our likes and dislikes as generated by conscious choice. It is a shock to realize that most of our so-called choices are dictated by the energetic qualities of our body.

It is as if we are riding on a machine made of varying combinations of the five material energies. Those combinations give rise to a body type that in turn acts and interacts with other combinations of matter in predictable ways. When you remember that everything in the realm of matter is simply made of some combination of the five elements, you will see the power of this model. It is the ultimate point and click user-interface between Nature and us.

The Five Elements in Your Daily Life

All foods and herbs are also composed of the same basic elemental characteristics. Some foods are heating, some are cooling, some are light, some are heavy and so on. In fact, every closed cycle of Nature is composed of moments in which one of the five elements is dominant. The day cycle, lunar cycle and year cycle surround us with a predictable fluctuation of elemental qualities. This is really useful science! If you know your permanent body type, you can predict the effect of living in a particular climate, season, time of month or time of day. You can also predict the result of eating certain food, taking specific herbs and living or working with a particular person.

Qualities of the Six Flavors

TASTE	ELEMENTS	ESSENCE	VATA	PITTA	KAPHA
Sweet	Earth/Water	Cold	Subdues	Subdues	Increases
Sour	Earth/Fire	Hot	Subdues	Increases	Increases
Salty	Water/Fire	Hot	Subdues	Increases	Increases
Pungent	Air/Fire	Hot	Increases	Increases	Subdues
Astringent	Air/Earth	Cold	Increases	Subdues	Subdues
Bitter	Air/Akasha	Cold	Increases	Subdues	Subdues

What is fairly obvious in weather is less obvious in the cycle of the day. Yet each day is simply a small set of seasonal manifestations of dark and light, heat and cold, wet and dry. The case with food is even subtler. According to Ayurvedic medicine, there are six different flavors in food: sweet, salty, sour, bitter, astringent and pungent. The mix of five elements creates the distinctive flavor of each food. The chart demonstrates the relationships between the five elements and the six flavors.

All foods fall into these six categories. With this understanding it is possible to respond both to the seasonal influences, time of day, time of month and also the inherent constitutional type. With this knowledge, you can eat scientifically for the first time in your life. With this new empowerment, Ayurvedic medicine answers the question that haunts modern medicine: "How do we prevent disease?" All disease takes place as a result of imbalances, which eventually create an internal climate that supports disease. Bacteria and viruses do not attack everyone because not everyone is in a state of imbalance.

Therefore, if people in general can learn to manage their diets with the advice of an ayurvedically trained doctor who monitors their state of balance, then for the first time in the history of the Western world we will have a tool for the large scale prevention of disease. This is predicated upon an understanding of the five-element body type. In fact, through the Vedic horoscope it is also possible to know when certain imbalances will manifest based on changing external cosmic rays due to planetary movements. Each piece of this powerful knowledge fits together with the others to produce a material science integrated into the dynamic processes of Nature. Now that the five elements are understood, it is necessary to discuss the three processes that manifest them over time.

Prime Numbers

Marks of distinction, strung in space
through time,
Someone did the math,
Geometry unfolding so sublime,
Every planet's path
Follows hidden markers in the sky,
Calculate the odds,
Randomness is illusion's greatest lie
In the war against the gods.
Three sides of a cube are always hidden,
Black side of the Moon,
Dark digits whose meaning is the forbidden
Ratio within the rune.
Earth, Sun and Moon in revolution,
Ratios so precise,
Pose a problem with only one solution,
God does not play dice!

Jeffrey Armstrong

Chapter Eight

The Three Gunas, or "What Ya Guna Do?"

The universe is always building us out of itself. As we discussed earlier, the matter of Nature can be seen in very complex ways that have been perfected by modern scientific methods. For complex manipulations of engineering, such minute knowledge is very exacting. On a day-to-day basis, it is actually too complex for us to use in deciding what to eat or what to do. We cannot easily recognize elements like copper, iron or zinc by looking at our body. The five elements, on the other hand, are really the five states of matter as we see it around us all the time. They are not competing models but two ways to see the same reality for different purposes. The solid, liquid, burning, subtle and spacious form our every perception.

Everything we perceive is made of some combination of these five. The ability to see them is a simple user-interface between ourselves and the objects that surround us. If your body is made of more fire and it is noon on a summer day, eating hot food and drinking alcohol would not be a good idea. This simple methodology turns out to be very practical once you learn the heating, cooling, drying and moistening properties of all the foods you might eat. It is an immediate tool for maintaining balance in an otherwise complicated world of choices. In Vedic astrology and Ayurvedic medicine, understanding those five elements is the basis of understanding the substance of matter.

In the World of Matter Everything Is Temporary

The companion of the five-element knowledge is called the *three gunas*. The gunas are about the three processes of matter: *creation, maintenance and destruction*. In modern scientific terms: *anabolism, metabolism and catabolism*, or building up, sustaining and breaking down.

The Taoist philosophers say, "The only constant is change." The modern laws of thermodynamics say the same thing differently. They state two laws: "Matter is neither created nor destroyed but merely changes form, and all matter is going from a higher state of energy to a lower state and in the process giving off both heat and waste." The last principle is called *entropy*. Because of entropy, everything is wearing out once it is created. Another way to state this occurs in the Chinese classic the *I Ching*, or *Book of Changes*: "A movement is accomplished in six stages, the seventh brings return." The Vedas also say matter goes through six stages of development: "It has a beginning, growth, duration, produces some by-products, withers and dies." All of these discuss the actions of the gunas, or three processes of matter.

Since matter is unconscious, everything that is born must die. That is the full impact of the law of entropy. When something is created, it has locked within it a certain amount of energy. Friction within matter wears at that original form and gradually wears it down. Since it is the nature of matter to be formless and unconscious, destruction is the easiest of the three processes. Next comes creation. The creative impulse is how everything comes into manifestation. It is intense, concentrated and highly focused. The most difficult life process is maintenance. For this reason, there is no such thing in Nature as a perpetual motion machine. In our bodies, these three processes are always going on simultaneously. When we are children, the creative force is most active, as a result we grow. As adults, we maintain ourselves as long as possible. Old age is simply the destructive process wearing out the body and its parts faster than they can be restored. The ancients called these the three gunas, or rulers, of Nature.

Matter transforms in five states from space to air to fire to water to earth. The movement is from subtle to dense, from invisible to solid. When things are created out of the five elements, they exist in the context of past, present and future. They contain within them the tendencies of the material element which predominates. Some have more earth and thus are heavier. Some have more fire and are more burning and intense. In addition to the density of the matter of which they are composed, they also have a predominating guna. Some are decomposing very rapidly, some are in the creative stage and some are maintaining for a time. If you apply this to human beings, we experience all three states over the course of our life. Take for example the creation of a child. Sex and the ensuing pregnancy takes only nine months, raising a child takes twenty years, damaging or killing a baby takes only a moment of neglect.

How Moral Values Arise from the Gunas

Because we understand this intuitively, we respect those who preserve life and create peace even more than we respect masters of the creative process like artists and entertainers or those with great energy. Those who needlessly or selfishly destroy life are generally considered bad. The three gunas are the operative principle behind ethics and morality. The three gunas are sometimes called goodness, passion and ignorance. What seems to be an impersonal and abstract process of Nature eventually appears as the qualities of value in everything that exists in Nature. You could say that every person or thing in life is a representative or embodiment of some combination of the three gunas.

Perhaps another way to express this is that we each contain all three gunas but one becomes our predominating guna. Thus, over the long run of our life we consistently act to create, maintain or destroy life. An example from our daily life would be a judge, a policeman and a criminal. The destructive acts of the criminal are a form of ignorance, malice or disregard for the sacredness of life, or *tamas*. The strength of the policeman is a form of creative passion, or *rajas*. The wisdom of the judge embodies the law, which is directed at maintaining life for all, which is *sattvic*. The policeman runs the risk of becoming tamasic by associating with too many criminals. If he associates with judges, priests, saints, and good people, his own sattva is strengthened. The secret of the gunas is that association strengthens our tendency to become like one or the other guna.

God Is the Creator, Maintainer and Destroyer

The Vedic view of God is that outside of matter the three gunas do not exist. Inside the material realm, God rules through these three processes. In a sense, each of the gunas is a manifestation of Divine Intelligence. In this world, all three are necessary. In the religion of the Vedas they are personified as *Brahma* the Creator, *Vishnu* the Maintainer and *Shiva* the Destroyer. These three were never conceived as three competing Gods but as three aspects of the one Supreme Being who is manifest in the past, present and future of material Nature. Think of the English word GOD as an acronym for: Generation, Organization and Destruction. Even though all three are necessary for life to exist in the realm of matter, the sustaining principle most clearly represents the ongoing Divine desire for the happiness and continuation of all life.

The guna which sustains is called *sattva*, the guna of creation is called *raja* and the guna of destruction is called *tamas*. You might say that, depending on the soul's level of illusion, one will forget one's true nature and become more and more immersed in matter. Since matter is dark and unconscious, the rule of tama guna is represented by the color black and sometimes dark blue. The creative guna, rajas, is in between. Its ability to create comes from unlimited desire and activity within matter. Red is the color associated with rajas. The Sanskrit term for a great king is *Maharaja*. Sattva is the most refined state of matter, where the soul is the least forgetful of its true nature. Its traditional color is white or yellow and sometimes gold.

A good way to remember the gunas is to associate them with the three primary colors: blue, red and yellow. Just as all colors are formed from those three primaries, so everything that exists in Nature is some combination of the three gunas. In Sanskrit, *guna* also means *rope*. They are the ties that bind the soul to matter. If you have a sattvic day, your mind is peaceful and enlightened. If you become rajasic, desire and activity become overwhelming and drive you without peace or rest. If tamas rules, you will feel depressed, lethargic and perhaps angry and destructive.

Every material thing is imbued with some proportion of all three gunas but the dominant guna gives it a particular quality. Whatever quality you associate with, your consciousness will take on. That is the secret of association. Every parent has seen this first hand. When a child is still forming, the result of good or bad association is very clear. Experiments have been performed with plants demonstrating that if you play violent music nearby, the plants will wither and die. People are the same. If you put them in sattvic and enlightening surroundings, they will reflect those qualities. The gunas are all around and within us. Since our body and mind are made of matter, both of them are also created in a particular guna.

This is where karma enters the picture. Through our actions in previous lives, we develop an accumulation of karmic reactions which travel with us in our body and mind as tendencies and habits. Some beings are born sattvic, some rajasic, some tamasic and all shades and combinations of the three. Guna, or quality, is inherent at birth but association can modify it. A person's guna is also identifiable in their Vedic astrological chart. This means you can see the level of moral and ethical development by examining the horoscope at birth.

The Three Gunas

Descriptive	State of Mind
SATTVA Goodness-Equilibrium-Metabolism-Integration-Maintenance-Organization-Sustaining-Supporting-Balance-Sustenance-Equipoise-Order-Consiousness-Union-Peace-Light	**SATTVA** Harmony: the mind's balanced state in which it discriminates correctly, clearly and accurately.
RAJAS Passion-Creation-Motion-Desire-Excitement-Urges-Longings-Appetite-Agitation-Hunger-Lust-Active-Ferment-Tumult	**RAJAS** Hankering: the state in which excessive mental activity weakens discrimination and clouds judgement.
TAMAS Ignorance-Destruction-Anger-Inertia-Disintegration-Lethargy-Darkness	**TAMAS** Lamentation: the state in which insufficient mental activity destroys discrimination.

The Gunas in Your Daily Life

In this world, the gunas surround us and are within us. They create the atmosphere of our times. Wartime is tamasic. A great renaissance is rajasic. Peacetime is sattvic. Our home also is either dirty (tamasic) or clean (sattvic), or somewhere in between. Our intentions are passionate, attached and driven; peaceful, loving and enlightene;, or ignorant, angry and destructive. Who we associate with always reinforces one of those tendencies.

Now let me give you an example of how the gunas could be used in a practical way to change our lives. Unfortunately, one of the biggest growth industries in America today is our prison systems. Obviously, these are places where we store people who have been judged "bad" by society. In fact, within prisons there is a core of very tamasic, or bad, people and then a larger group of rajasic persons who ended up in prison because of a difficult time in their life.

The question is: What is the purpose of a prison? It is a well-known fact that your average professional criminal considers prison "college"—a place he can expect to spend at least eight years of life getting a Ph.D. in tamas. This is because the bad (destructive energy) rules in prisons. How else could it be that drugs and alcohol are so available in prisons? Obviously, the rajasic prisoners will become more tamasic by association with the bad in such a destructive environment.

Using the knowledge of the gunas, another kind of prison system could be possible. We could: paint the prisons a soothing pastel color, feed the prisoners a strictly vegetarian diet, allow no smoking, drugs or alcohol for guards or inmates, play calming music throughout the prison, allow no violent movies or television shows, and implement training in non-violent restraint for guards. In other words, as far as possible, the prison would be kept sattvic.

Modalities of Nature

Activity	Sattva	Rajas	Tamas
ATTACHMENT TO GUNA	Happiness & Wisdom	Action & Desire	Ignorance & Laziness
INCREASE OF GUNA	Enlightenment	Restlessness	Delusion
EFFECT OF GUNA	Harmony	Pain	Distress
DIRECTION	Upward	Middle	Downward
WORSHIP	The Supreme	The Gods	The Demons
FOOD	Vegetable	Animal	Decaying
SACRIFICE	As Duty	For Result	For Wrong
AUSTERITY	For Purity	For Recognition	As Self Torture
SPEECH	Sweet & Truthful	Clever & Manipulating	Harsh & Lying
STATE OF MIND	Peaceful	Agitated	Tormented
CHARITY	For Right Cause	For Benefit	To the Unworthy
MOTIVE OF RENUNCIATION	For Higher Knowledge	From Sorrow	From Fear
RELIGIOUS VISION	God in All	God in Some	No God
MODE OF ACTION	Without Attachment	With Much Effort	Causing Harm
SELF EXPRESSION	Refined & Elegant	Impassioned	Vulgar & Distorted
POWER OF REASONING	Calm & Clean	Disturbed by Desires	Perverse & Distorted
MOTIVE FOR ACTION	Universal Well-being	Selfish Attachment	Stupidity & Despair
SOURCE OF PLEASURE	Greater Good	Pleasure to the Senses	Chaos & Pain
GOAL AFTER DEATH	Higher Realms	Actions on Earth	Realms of Darkness

According to the laws of Nature, the bad (destructive/tamasic) people would hate this prison environment because it would weaken the bad in them. The rajasic prisoners would become more sattvic and thus be improved. In this way, we would truly punish the bad with goodness and improve the rest. Otherwise, our current program is tamasic ruled by tamas and rajas. The result is that graduates of our current prison system learn to be more tamasic. We could improve society simply by understanding the gunas.

In coming chapters, we are going to see how the entire universe uses the five elements and three gunas to create, maintain and destroy all of life. Vedic astrology gives one the ability to use the moment of birth in order to extract information about the elemental construction and gunic qualities, which the atma or soul has accrued through its previous life actions. Scientists are interested in speculating and debating about how the stars and planets cause the creation of all beings at the beginning of time. Unfortunately, they have missed the more obvious and important correlation between the stars and behavior, which is visible at birth.

The horoscope created by the moment of birth is a device that allows us to recognize patterns of cause and effect and the direction that that cause and effect will take. This also means the planets and stars must be able to manifest or indicate some proportionate amount of the influence of the five elements and three gunas. In other words, each planet will represent a manifestation of rajasic, sattvic or tamasic energy. Each will also indicate the proportions of space, air, fire, water and earth that comprise our being, since those elements are the basic building blocks of the universe. I suspect that there must be many unexplored connections between the periodic table of elements and the genetic code of modern science and the planets and stars. That is a mystery which would interest me if I were a physicist, biologist or astronomer!

I Am the Subject

In the sentence of life which we project,
I am the subject and mine is the object.
Time is the ocean, space is the land,
We are the countless grains of sand
Which through the gate of life must pass,
A flow in illusion's hour glass.
There is no origin of the verb "to be"
All beginnings are shrouded in mystery
And as our essences intertwine,
The point circles to a spiral line.
A double helix dark and light,
Encrypted forms that make our sight,
Orbit, appearing to be outside,
The cave where we in darkness hide
And clinging to objects, become subject
To matter's laws, we don't suspect
That in our objects we are lost.
I am the subject was the cost.

Jeffrey Armstrong

Chapter Nine

The Self That Can't Be Killed

For many years now I have thought of Vedic astrology as the foothills of a great range of mountains. A discussion of how the Divine Intelligence behind life interacts with us leads inevitably to the greatest spiritual questions—questions that tower above us like peaks of an inaccessible mountain range. The power of Vedic astrology is its abilty to measure otherwise invisible movements of energy as they pertain to each individual. That perspective of acknowledging the invisible Divine Intelligence causes an important shift in our behavior. We become accountable.

Accountability is the real issue on our planet. It is not technology per se that is causing the destruction of our world but rather the selfish and irresponsible use of the new powers of technology. You might well argue, as many do, that since we are all individual selves, why not take whatever we want and be totally selfish. The Vedic answer to that question is a vision of self which serves our selfish needs and also serves the higher purpose of life.

Vedic astrology is a discussion of the current condition of the eternal self as it uses free will in the context of matter. In the

Vedas, astrology is intimately connected to theology, the nature of God, which in turn is connected to the true nature and purpose of the self. In Sanskrit, the term for our *true self* is *atma*. In English, the word soul comes close. The word *atom* is derived from *atma*. Just as the smallest piece of matter is called an atom, so our *irreducible self* is called the *atma*. Atma is the inner you who is the source of the consciousness that animates your mind and body. Think of your body and the bodies of all living things as light bulbs, each with a different capacity and all sustained by an atma that generates the electricity of consciousness.

How You See "Self" Has a Critical Impact on How You Act

The Vedas say that according to our past actions, we have developed a particular body, which is both our advantage and our limitation. At the core of that body is an eternal, indestructible spark of the Divine—of God. That core self is your eternal being. Once that spark enters into matter, it forgets its original nature and identifies self as the body and mind. In that consciousness, souls covered by matter act and, if they are humans, reap the fruits of their actions. Animals, plants, insects and all the rest are not generating karma through their actions, even though they too are eternal souls.

Humans, on the other hand, are able to act from free will and can generate considerable reaction to what they do. Therefore, how humans view their *self* has a critical impact on how they act. An animal acts according to its nature, no meditation is necessary. But according to the Vedas, humans have to learn of the atma, their true self which has been forgotten, or they will act unconsciously like an animal, simply in the habits of the body. One difference is animals are not greedy. They eat, sleep, protect and mate according to their immediate need, under the compulsion of their particular bodily nature. Humans can create huge problems by getting out of balance in the mind, body and soul relationship. Look at our culture and ask yourself how much time we devote to the body each day, how much to the mind and how much to the atma. Clearly, the atma has been left out. Could that be related to the imbalance we have created in the world?

Realizing that you are the atma is not just a religious subject based on faith and pertaining to the future. It is not that the soul is a future topic important only when the body is dead. The atma is the true center and correct definition of who we are that sets up the correct context of our present action.

This is where science without a sacred viewpoint simply creates sophisticated animals capable of causing more damage. In fact, learning to see the invisible is the real art of living. Helen Keller is said to have observed: "I believe in the immortality of the soul because I have within me immortal longings." Vedic astrology recognizes (1) the invisible atma, (2) the invisible Divine helpers in Nature, and last of all: (3) the Invisible Paramatma, the Supreme Soul—God. In the Vedas, the relationship between these three is the basis of true enlightenment. Vedic astrology serves to explain the links of cause and effect that unite all these components into a complete and provable science. Astrological guidance is meant to make clear the relation between the atma, the forces of Nature and the Supreme Being.

Vedic knowledge is unique in many ways. One of its most valuable contributions is an extensive vocabulary of technical spiritual terms. Just as the computer age has added thousands of new words to our technical vocabulary, so the golden age of spiritual research thousands of years ago created a special vocabulary of spiritual terms in the precise and highly specialized Sanskrit language. Initiation into Vedic knowledge requires acquiring a vocabulary of these technical terms, since there are no equivalent words in English or other European languages. Indeed, most of these concepts are so subtle that there are no words for them even in Latin or Greek. Words like *guru, karma* and *pundit* are examples of our culture adopting such Sanskrit technical terms. I am purposely keeping them to a minimum in this book to keep it generally accessible.

The Eternal Qualities of the Atma

In order to understand the atma better, it is necessary to introduce four more Sanskrit terms that refine our understanding beyond the vague English word soul. According to the Vedas, atma is composed of four qualities. The first is *sat*, or *eternality*. The soul was never created and never dies. Once the atma is covered with matter and has a material body, it experiences the illusion of death as bodies are born, age and die. The atma is unborn and undying.

The next is *chit*, which means *made of consciousness or knowledge*. We are used to thinking of knowledge as something that comes from outside to inside our awareness. It is true that knowledge of matter and its laws is alien to our original nature. Since we are not made of matter, we must learn of it from an outside source. Material knowledge is also lost for the most part, from life to life. However, in our original condition as the soul, we are fully conscious with no need for sleep and no interruption in our knowing. The atma has its own special senses for knowing which are inconceivable from the dualistic view of material understanding.

The third quality of the atma is *ananda*, or *bliss*. You could also translate *ananda* as *ecstasy*. If matter is static and unconscious, then atma is ecstatic. The point here is that soul is by nature joyful, or in a state of constant pleasure. In the realm of matter we are conditioned to think of pleasure and pain as two sides of a coin. We cannot easily imagine a state of pure bliss that is not defined and limited by pain and suffering, yet that is the Vedic definition of our true nature when it is unaffected by the dullness of matter.

The last definition of self is *vigraha*, which means *distinctive individuality*. The reason we have appeared as materialized individuals with free will is that our true self has an eternal form of individuality that is not dependent upon matter for its distinctiveness. This kind of precise spiritual understanding is characteristic of Vedic knowledge. It is the substructure that supports the higher capabilities and insights of Vedic astrology.

Paramatma, the Supreme Soul

Paramatma, the *Supreme Soul*, is the founder of the whole system of karma. The planets serve the Supreme Intelligence by controlling the dispersal of action and reaction upon the Earth. The numerous atmas act, creating the need for an appropriate response which they finally experience as happiness or distress. As you can see, souls are poised between two great realities: Paramatma and Material Nature, God and the unconscious material shadow of God. Nature is made of the inert and unconscious substances of matter as we have observed. Souls are conscious by nature, which explains their frustration with matter. No one wants birth, death, old age and disease. Given a choice, the atma would prefer not to be limited by those forces.

Eventually, after enough experience in matter, the atma explores the possibility of returning to the spiritual realm that is its original home. The potential for that leaving begins by a change in the definition of self. If you see yourself as an eternal soul temporarily in the realm of matter, you will act very differently than someone who believes they are merely a human animal with only one birth. At that point, the awareness dawns that really winning the game is not being forced to play the game under the limitations of matter. That state of eternal freedom which begins with a redefinition of the material self as the eternal self, or atma, is called *liberation*, or in the Sanskrit: *Mukti*.

Mukti means *returning to our original consciousness which is non-material*. If you die in that consciousness, you do not take another material body. Souls who have gotten free return to the realms of spiritual life from which they originally came. The effect of this redefinition of self on material living is that it becomes less driven and greedy. In the words of the American transcendentalist David Thoreau: "Simple living and high thinking." In Bharata (India), Vedic astrology is also called *Jyotisha*, or the *Science of Light*. Light originates in the same eternal place where we originated. Yoga is the process of returning to and reconnecting with our source. Vedic astrology is the art and science of understanding how the world of matter is regulated and directed by Divine beings working within the light. The whole cycle of action and result over time in the context of Divine Intelligence is called karma, the core subject of Vedic astrology.

Time Is a Snake

Time is a snake
On a placid lake,
Reflecting an endless sky,
With a curving motion
That churns the ocean,
His coils are the years that fly.
Like a falcon's flight
Toward the rising light
Of a golden eternal Sun,
Racing through space
With a shining face,
Where sunbeams are everyone.
And above that lagoon
The rising Moon
Weaves a web of silver strands,
Like a spider of pearl,
They drape and curl,
From her spinning and delicate hands.
On the firmament
Glistening orbs are bent
Into shapes of subtle design,
In a secret code,
Like a hidden road,
That leads us to the Divine.
And the snake's direction
Across the reflection
Sends ripples that touch the shore,
Which shapes the sand,
Like a pattern planned,
That has never been seen before.

Jeffrey Armstrong

Chapter Ten

Free Will Creates Karma and Destiny

In India and most Eastern countries, astrology has always been connected to a view of the individual self as an eternal entity. This is the basis of the free will/destiny discussion, which often arises when people hear of astrology. The real underlying question is: "Who am I?" The answer we choose for this question sets the context of our life. Our options are one of the three following conclusions. In the first, we identify with our body as self and when it is gone so are we—end of story. In the second, we believe we have the potential to be divine and someone outside of our self has the power to grant us eternal life in some way or another. In the third, we are eternal beings by nature and will always be so, even if we temporarily forget. Once accepted, these three views of who we are act as a context, or worldview, which constantly surrounds us and influences many of our decisions, consciously and unconsciously.

The first view is essentially atheistic. My favorite definition of this view is "An atheist is someone with no invisible means of support." People have often presented themselves in this way to avoid the pressures of organized religions. Setting that aside, the deeper question is whether or not the universe is supported by the actions of an intelligent and loving conscious being. Many people feel frustrated by the brutality of death or the immensity of the universe and also embrace an agnostic conclusion. The negative side of life seems to argue in favor of an empty or cynical view that despairs over any continued existence of the self. Although the cynics who hold this view believe in cause and effect, that belief does not lead them to experience either a Divine Intelligence or their own divinity. To the atheistic mind, astrology would only be believable as material cause and effect.

The Catholics Remove the Soul

The second group is found mostly in the Judaic, Christian and Islamic traditions. For example, most people are unaware that reincarnation or the pre-existence of the soul was a much-debated topic for the first 400 years of Christianity. All the people in the debate considered themselves Christian. To some, the idea that the soul was eternal and had many births made the most sense of Jesus' message of love. This group argued that since God loves us and sent his son Jesus to teach love, it would be more loving for the soul to have many opportunities than to be limited to only one birth. However, in the 5th century, during the Nicene Councils held by the Roman Catholic Church, the idea of reincarnation was voted out. The final result was a view that the soul does not pre-exist before the birth of the body.

This view of the proximate creation of the soul concurrent with individual human sexual conception became dogma in the Catholic Church and remains so to this day. There was a time not too long ago that you could be put to death for the "Eastern heresy" of believing in or teaching reincarnation. Whatever the Church's motives were, the result was more control over people who were not allowed to believe that their soul was by nature eternal. The Church would only confer immortality if you behaved properly; it was their power over you. Needless to say, since true astrology is based on a pre-existing soul and reincarnation, the Christian view of astrology has not been very favorable. It is also worth remembering that the Three Wise Men who visited Jesus at his birth were Persian astrologers. They knew from the planetary positions that a great soul was taking birth.

The third viewpoint is that the soul, or core self, is eternal and never dies. That an eternal individual self is the core around which we have built our mind and body is the basis of Vedic astrology. You could say that the soul is our true self, encased inside a diving suit made of matter. That diving suit is a creation of our own actions. In other words, it is the result of our karma. *Karma* is a Sanskrit word which means *to do*. Whatever we do in matter creates a reaction, since "Every action has an equal and opposite reaction." In this view, there are three things to understand: God, the multitude of living beings and the organization of Nature. This means Vedic astrology is a sub-science of Vedic religion and science. It is all about the long-term cause and effect relationship between souls and God and what happens to souls while they exercise free will in the material world.

There is a famous verse in the *Parasara Hora*, a Vedic astrological text that explains the relation of astrology to the notion of God. The verse says: "The function of the planets is to give the many souls their karma on behalf of God." In other words, God created Nature; Nature has certain rules which give rise to cause and effect. The souls are forced to accept the pleasant or unpleasant results of their actions by the planets who act as messengers of God. You could say the planets are Angels cooperating with God in order to maintain order in a universe where free will is allowed. The use of free will will cause a continuous stream of reactions.

Here is a good way to understand karma. What exactly were you doing on this day twenty years ago? It is unlikely you can remember; yet, you were doing something. The things you did in the past have already reshaped who you are. Some of the reactions to your actions may still be coming toward you, for good or bad. That process of reaction over time is called karma. It is obvious that we are constantly forgetting or are unaware of the subtle effects of our actions. In spite of our forgetfulness, there is an Intelligence in Nature that remembers what we do. If this is true in one lifetime of our action and forgetfulness, then because of our eternal nature, the same principle is at work from lifetime to lifetime. If we are the soul and the soul is eternal, then it is probable that those reactions follow us from life to life until they are used up or somehow removed.

Karma, the Secret of Free Will

This is the secret of free will and the Vedic long-term view of justice. When we exercise our free will within the rules of material Nature, we are given feedback, a reaction. We experience those reactions as good or bad because they give us pleasure or pain. Ultimately, they are all good since they are part of a system which allows freedom of action and choice. That freedom of action is our soul's opportunity to evolve to its highest level. You might say we are constantly using free will in the context created from our past use of free will. Imagine for a moment that the core self is a non-material, non-destructible essence.

Picture yourself in a diving suit deep at the bottom of the ocean. The suit you are wearing is the physical body, which is made of the five elements and three gunas: earth, water, fire, air and space, and rajas, tamas and sattva. Underneath that suit is a subtler layer of energy which includes the mind and intellectual functions. The Vedas call the physical body the *waking body*. When we are awake, we identify our self with the physical body. When we sleep, the physical body is inactive but we continue to live and experience life in our *subtle body*. The Vedas call that our *dream body*.

The physical body is like a coat and the dream body is like a shirt. Underneath those two is the permanent self, or soul, the atma. Karma is the changes in the physical and mental bodies, which result from our use of free will in the context of universal law. This means that at any given time we have a backlog of reactions which the universe owes us. When those reactions arrive, we will experience them as pleasant or unpleasant. They will make us happy or unhappy. In the bigger picture, they are as impersonal as the flame that burns us. If you place your hand in the fire, it does not ask if you are bad or good. It simply burns according to its own nature. Karma is an impersonal reaction to our actions within matter.

Suitcases of Karma

Picture the birth of a child as the next step of manifestation in the eternal life of a soul. This soul chose to live for the time being in the material ocean. At birth, it is as if an airplane lands and drops a passenger off at his or her destination, the home of a new set of parents. Those parents and their material circumstances are the next unfoldment of that soul's karma, or destiny. It is a payback—a fulfilling of previous conditions and, in some ways, a choosing. While the child is landing, the suitcases are unloaded from the plane and stored in the basement of the home. On the bags is a sign which reads: "Do not open until you leave home."

We all can remember the transition from our time at home to living on our own. It is the moment when we take back the right to make all our own choices. That choosing is a combination of new choice (free will) and the resources that we already have (karma). Vedic astrology is based on the premise that the points of light in the sky at the moment of birth are capable of revealing information about the patterns of karma that are still stored in the suitcases. The sky is like an electronic scoreboard at a sporting event. If you can read the signs in the sky, you will know a partial readout of the karma carried by any soul.

Three Kinds of Karma

The word karma is a much-misunderstood word. According to the Vedas, there are three kinds of karma that we carry with us at any time. The first is bearing fruit now; that is called *prarabda*, or *already ripe fruit*. Who your parents are, your country of birth, brothers and sisters, your marriage partner and children, your body type, gender, genetics, blood type. None of these can be changed significantly. These are already decided at birth. To fight against them is almost impossible because they are already the ripe fruit of your past action. There are other karmas coming toward you at the present moment that are unstoppable. That is your destiny. Nothing you do can prevent their arrival. Only an act of God could stop them. I call these the pizzas you have ordered and their delivery is the *Cosmic Domino* effect.

God is the creator of the system, so at any point Divine Intervention is the wild card in the deck. Failing that, they will arrive. Many times those karmas are visible in the horoscope and can be seen in advance by an astrologer. Some karma that is in the fruit stage can be modified through knowledge and new action but usually only within certain narrow boundaries.

The second kind of karma is in the seedling stage. It is called *sanchitta. Those karmic seeds are stored or contained in our mind as the tendencies accumulated from past experiences.* Unaltered they will grow into actions and resultant reactions. For this reason, yoga and many processes of self-improvement focus upon changing the mind. Imagine the mind as a mirror covered with dust. The color and nature of the dust depends on where you have been. That covering of dust is your karmic seeds planted from past actions. That dust colors your view of reality. It tints all your perceptions. Eventually those tints will lead you to certain conclusions and actions, which will finally give certain results (karma).

If you could remove that dust from your mind, your mind would become clear and the tendencies to certain kinds of karma would be removed. In other words, you can burn karma off your mind or soul through certain processes of purification. You can actually remove and exhaust the supply of past karma. In that case, the suitcases of karma would eventually be empty. That liberated state where no karma remains is one of the goals of yogic practice.

That leads us to the third type of karma, which is called *kriyamana*, or *action without generating reaction*. Have you noticed that a war hero is given a medal for killing hundreds of people whereas someone who does the same thing for selfish reasons is put in jail? The action is the same: killing. The result is very different. Souls acting for their own selfish purposes are subject to the reactions of their deeds, good or bad. However, if a soul becomes sufficiently evolved to act completely in the service of God, he or she would no longer generate—or be controlled by— karma. In other words, at a certain level of growth, we escape cause and effect and enter directly into Divine service. At that time, no more karma is created by our actions.

There is a story about a yogi who once sat on a rock for ten years, praying to God to appear before him. Finally God appeared in the form of Vishnu. God spoke to the yogi and offered him any boon he would like. The yogi replied that he would like justice. Vishnu answered that he had many better things to offer which would be much more enjoyable. The yogi was adamant that he only wanted justice. Finally, in frustration, Vishnu said: "Alright, may the rock now sit on you for ten years!"

This raises the next question: "Who or what in Nature is giving us the reactions of our karma from day to day and life to life?" Every answer to such an ultimate question comes to us as a description of something we cannot completely see. We are surrounded by a mysterious universe, which feeds and cares for us in ways that cannot be understood by scientific explanations of the outward processes. The ultimate questions of life are about its purpose, not merely its process. Again, Vedic astrology is a bridge between the realms of visible and invisible reality.

GOD the CEO

You might say light is the external manifestation of an unseen internal reality. Just as our eyes only see the visible spectrum of light, so we as residents within matter see only the visible part of the universe. It is only a partial view. According to Veda, at least three-quarters of the true process of life is invisible. The question of cause and effect is actually the question of whether or not the Cosmos is pervaded by Divine Intelligence. If you were the president of a large and powerful corporation, would you personally sweep the floors, ship the products and type the letters, or would you delegate that work to thousands of employees in your hire?

In the Vedic view, the universe is just such a cooperative venture. In a way you could say God is the CEO who creates directives of Divine Intelligence by which creation, maintenance and destruction are made possible. That process is conducted by a group of angelic souls known in Sanskrit as Devas (those who work in the light), who work directly for God in the execution of the Divine processes which sustain life. Life is an arrangement of energetic potential that provides an opportunity for countless souls to experience their individuality in the context of the actions and reactions of matter. The planets and stars represent the distributed authority of God. Thus, it is that the planets and stars, who are also Devas, give us our karma, acting on behalf of God.

Midsummer Night's Eve

The solstice gate
Is open late,
Burning all night in the sky,
When the northern course
Is a racing horse
And the souls of enlightenment fly.
In the violet space
Shines another place,
The capital city of light,
With ramparts of fire,
The wise aspire
To taste its ambrosial delight.
In the middle of summer,
The dark ones slumber,
Unable to open their eyes
But the blessed awake
And meet near a lake
In the gardens of paradise.
Inside that portal,
The nectar immortal,
Is poured into ivory bowls,
While a feast made of truth,
Brings back sweetness and youth,
To their dancing and laughing souls.
From that glistening chalice,
The Aurora Borealis
Drifts down the shimmering air,
Like a curtain of grace
Made of sparkling lace,
It hints at the pleasure they share.
On midsummer night's eve,
Each flower and leaf,
Blooms in anticipation
And prays for a hand
To weave them a garland,
In the Devas' divine celebration.

Jeffrey Armstrong

Chapter Eleven

Devas, the Angels Who Direct Air-Traffic Control

At the center of our solar system the Sun shines its light, providing us with the energy that creates and sustains life. Our other great light, the Moon, delivers a cooler reflected form of that light energy. The movements of the Moon are connected to the waters that nurture life, controlling the tides and influencing plant growth. The closest planets—Mercury, Venus, Mars, Jupiter and Saturn—can be seen to move through the sky. The Greeks called them *the wanderers* for that reason. In Sanskrit, they are called *Graha*, which means to *grab or grasp*. Through their power they reach out and grasp our lives. Graha is the root word of the English word gravity. Unlike the Sun and Moon, we cannot as easily see a physical connection between the planets and our daily life. Even more remote to our perception are the stars, which seem to decorate the sky, creating a distant backdrop to our lives.

Perceiving the Invisible Forces of Nature

It is only very recently that we have developed instruments sensitive enough to perceive invisible cosmic rays constantly reaching us from space. We have also finally proven that the very tiny sub-cellular structures of our bodies are profoundly influenced by small, almost unmeasurable, amounts of energy and magnetic resonance. Interestingly enough, that was exactly the premise of ancient seers and astrologers—that invisible cosmic rays were constantly in contact with us, even though we could not directly perceive their effects. In that way you could say that the conclusion of both astrology and modern science is that we are being transformed by interactions with invisible forces.

In spite of that agreement, there is one very important difference between ancient science and modern science. Ancient science is the study of how Nature works, with an assumption that our intelligence is a small part of a greater Intelligence which pervades all of Nature. That is the first assumption of sacred science. Modern science arose in the context of a religious culture that had wedded certain limited views of the physical world to the premise that the universe is intelligent. In order to remove those religious dogmas, science threw God out the window to gain freedom from Christian dogmatism. That became both its strength and limitation.

On the one hand, atheistic science tended to reduce all of life to mechanical material explanations. It did create a great focus on the physical and fostered huge advances in our ability to manipulate the physical world. Science can answer questions of how the universe operates down to a very minute level, but questions as to why the universe operates and questions of ultimate purpose are out of the grasp of science by definition.

The Intelligence Behind the Universe

Personally, I do not understand how one could study life without seeing it as the result of the action of a great

Intelligence. It would translate to "I, who am the greatest intelligence in Nature, am studying Nature, which is ignorant, even though Nature produced my intelligence." Doesn't that strike you as arrogant? I understand that certain dogmatic views have sometimes traveled with religion, but if you don't acknowledge the Intelligence which created the Cosmos, you are throwing the baby out with the bath water. Not only is it arrogant, it is also ignorant. It ignores the obvious intelligence required to create Nature. In any case, sacred science is based on the assumption that life is intelligent and directed by a purposeful intelligence. In Eastern thinking this made it easy to understand the notion of Divine helpers, or Devas.

All the World's a Stage

Picture the universe as the playing field for a great sporting event. The event is sponsored or initiated by someone. That is God, the Divine Will or Supreme Intelligence. On the playing field there are two groups of beings: the players (including the audience) and the stadium workers. The workers are working for the promoter. They have given up a certain amount of free will in order to serve in a specific way, which makes the event possible. They are always carrying out the will of God. You could call them the Angels, though often in Western religions Angels don't appear to have specific material tasks. The Devas, or Demi-gods if you like, all have specific jobs in the management of the material world. This means that behind the laws of matter, or its movement, invisible entities are working as a network of distributed intelligence. Their purpose is to maintain this material world on behalf of God so that we can act here on the playing field of life.

Imagine the countless billions of souls who are living in the realm of matter as players in an immense game. Remember that they are eternal and cannot die. Their origin is in another place which is not material. But somehow they have stepped onto the material playing field. When they do, they are exercising choice

121

or free will. By investing that free will they create karma which generates a certain body. Again, the body is like a light bulb. All souls have the same potential, but how that potential is manifested in matter at any time is limited by the bulb (body). Consciousness is the electrical current that animates the body. By using free will, the souls decide to become players (humans) or audience (plants and animals) or they are given a job working for the promoter (as Devas).

Vedic astrology is the science that tries to study the cause-and-effect relationship between the players and the stadium employees and, ultimately, the promoter. In between God and the players, the Devas act as referees. Some of those Devas are the planets and constellations whose outward appearance and position are the indicators of an invisible expression of Divine will and purpose. Thus, through the enforcement of karma, the Devas direct the game of life. You can't play tennis without a net, and—ultimately—someone is keeping score!

Dancing in the Light

The main difference between this view and that of modern science is the assumption that the rules of life are connected to intelligences that are actively interested in the outcome of the game. The opposite term for Deva is Asura. *Deva* means *playing in the light*, or *regulating life with light on behalf of God. Asura* means *against the light*. In Sanskrit, *a* means *not* and *sura* means *light (or good)*. Any player who is in the game but is against the rules of the game is "bad." They are trying to cheat or subvert the game of life by substituting their own self-made rules for the actual rules of Nature. In this, the Devas are the best scientists, since they know the laws of matter and are using them in the service of, or the intention of, the Divine desire.

If you want to become an Angel, first you must recognize the Supreme Intelligence. Then you must want to work in the service of that Intelligence. If you want to be a good player, you must learn to cooperate with the referees. Vedic astrology is the expression of the desire to understand the movements of the invisible intelligence in Nature and the desire to work and move or play cooperatively with them. It is the Devic desire to use our free will so that we play the game with the minimum of damage to the field and other players. Those who play fair get "good karma," while those who break the rules get "bad karma." What goes around (planets) comes around (gives you feedback on how you are playing the game).

Scientists of all varieties ask the question: "How does the Universe work?" The Devas' reply to their question is: "Why do you want to know?" If the answer is to participate in harmony with the Divine Intelligence, science will lead to being a Deva. If the desire is selfish, an unwillingness to play with the Divine, that science will lead to becoming an Asura.

In Vedic astrology, the desire is to understand our relationship with the Devas and their function of dispensing invisible waves of karma. Some knowledge of that relationship is revealed in the horoscope, as it is a record of the patterns of light at the moment of birth and their subsequent unfoldment. Once again, Vedic astrology is a science that operates with one foot in the realm of the soul and one in the realm of cause and effect in matter. In order to appreciate the meaning of free will and destiny, we need to explore the Eastern concept of self, or atma, further.

As Above, So Below

The Sun in the South
With an upturned mouth
Smiled across smoke and mist,
Like a flame in the snow
It began to grow
As it sank down into the West.
While the night hung back
Like a robe of black
Dropped on the Milky Way breast,
Of the curving lines,
On a form designed
In the place where two lovers had kissed.
And that airy embrace
Traced by light in space
Rose up on elliptical paths,
Descending above,
Intersections of love
Spilled down through celestial baths.
Down rivers of blue,
Past comets that flew
Like eagles to peaks far away,
Their love formed a stream,
Moving shapes in a dream
Overflooding the Earth night and day.
And the planets all turning
In the grip of that yearning
Spun madly in gravity's grip,
Like drunkards on wine,
They watched the divine
Lovers in space lip to lip.
Next a star broke apart
With a flash, from the heart
Of the pair whose passion increased,
And the heat of their souls
Shifted the poles,
While the Sun returned to the East.
Now racing toward spring
Where the Dragon will sing
To the Phoenix renewing her glow,
Then the Moon and the Sun
Merged together as one,
As above, so below.

Jeffrey Armstrong

Chapter Twelve

As Above, So Below
The Cosmos Within Your Body

Astrology is a living tradition in Bharata. It is part of a very ancient vision of our relation to the source of everything and the very immanent expression of Divine intent and intelligence in our everyday life. We believe either that we live in an empty, meaningless universe with no loving plan, or we acknowledge the constant efforts of an intelligent and loving Being who surrounds us in all we do.

There is no final proof in scientific terms. No one will prove either view to your mind's complete satisfaction. This is a decision you must make alone in the privacy of your own heart. With either choice, everything will change. Think of yourself as a planet like the Earth on which we live. What you call belief is in reality a choice and an expression of desire. If you do not see Divine Intelligence all around you, that is a choice. That's why no one can force you to see. You will only close your eyes tighter.

What if a cell in your body decided that it had no connection to anything greater and that there was no plan? How would your immune system view that conclusion? Here on Earth's body we also have a choice: Work with the purpose of preserving life or act in complete isolated selfishness. In one case, we will become a cancer cell, part of a tumor which denies the intelligence of the body. In the other case, we may become a T cell in the body of Earth which seeks to defend the whole system. Life is about choice. Extend that view to the solar system. It obviously is a system, whose purpose and method are hidden from our view. We can either assume it is intelligent or think of it as empty and ignorant. This truth extends to each new level of the totality.

Looking for Intelligence in All the Wrong Places

Why do you think we are overly concerned at this point in time with aliens? If someone drove up to your house in a fancy car, a Ferrari, would you bow down to him or her and think they were superior to you. Would you bow to the engineer of the car? Would you make them your teacher and learn how to live every area of your life from them? So why be preoccupied with aliens and going out into space? Are we searching for intelligence? Will you bow to the creator of a space ship just because they crossed the galaxy in a fancy car? Would that qualify them to teach you the meaning of life? Or are the answers to the deeper questions of life inside us?

Are we looking for intelligence in the wrong place? Is it because we don't trust ourselves to go within and make direct contact with higher intelligence? Vedic astrology, yoga and the real intention of religion all say that each individual must go within to make a meaningful connection with the underlying purpose of life. We are all cells in the body of God, each with equal access to the source of our own being.

During the Roman and early Christian period of history, the practice of astrology was often punishable by death. We have all lived in this intimidating atmosphere for many lifetimes. Our recent steps toward supporting free thought and speech are still tenuous advances against the violence people have faced for holding certain beliefs. The Roman emperors feared someone would know their future through astrology and use it as a power over them. The Christians saw astrologers as competition for the credibility of their followers.

The result for astrology was that it became viewed as a form of superstition or entertainment. It lost its connection to the stars, and it lost the underlying religious and empowering significance it had had originally. Right now, more great knowledge has been forgotten than is being remembered. If we diverted half the money from the space program to retrieving great wisdom that has been lost or forgotten, it would be a greater benefit to the world. Then we could have a space program and a grace program.

The Universe Is God's Body

Fortunately, Indian culture has kept some semblance of its traditions of five to ten thousand years ago alive. That was a time when spiritual knowledge had a great renaissance, just as material knowledge is having one at the present time. Modern science has a premise that the laws of matter are the same throughout the universe. Ancient sacred science had a similar conclusion, that the entire universe is a body created by God and that we are all cells in that great body. The secret of the human body is that all the primary principles of the Cosmos have been reproduced in the male and female body.

Since we are a miniature version of the whole, we contain within our structure all the principles on which the larger body was produced. Energy is flowing throughout our bodies, as in the Cosmos. We are constructed of the five elements and three gunas. Also the stars and planets exist both outside us and within us. As they move through space, they also move within us. The planets and stars are Devas and represent the Divine Will.

They are not in competition with God. They are each in charge of a domain within matter, which also means they are within us.

As the World Churns

There is an ancient Vedic story that illustrates how cosmology is related to biology. According to the Vedas, the endless universes are created, maintained and then destroyed in an endless cycle throughout all eternity. When they are created, all beings are reawakened from their slumber to resume their activities according to their previous desires and actions. The creator of each universe is a being known as Lord Brahma. With his feminine counterpart, Saraswati, he mentally creates the bodies for all the primary living entities. They are divided into two groups, the Devas and the Asuras.

The Devas embrace light and the Asuras embrace the dark. In order to continue the creative process, the two groups of beings decided to churn a great ocean of milk that covered the Cosmos. They used a mountain named Mandara as the churning rod and a serpent named Vasuki as the rope for churning. Lord Vishnu, who is God, appeared as a turtle swimming in the milk in order to support the mountain to facilitate the great churning.

The Asuras grasped the head of the serpent and the Devas its tail and they began to churn. Just as churning milk produces butter, churning this cosmic ocean produced many valuable items. The Moon arose from its depths, a horse with seven heads, a white elephant with four heads, valuable jewels arose from its depths, the goddess of all fortune, Lakshmi, came forth in splendor.

Finally, a divine being named Dhanvantari walked up onto the shore carrying a golden pot encrusted with jewels. In that pot was the nectar of immortality, ambrosia that would confer immortality upon anyone who drank it. The divine drink was known as *amrita*. Immediately the Devas and the Asuras rushed to the spot to obtain the precious liquid. But before they could begin to fight, Lord Vishnu the preserver again appeared in their midst as a beautiful woman named Mohini. Her beauty was so amazing that anyone who beheld her was immediately brought under her sway.

She instructed the Devas to form one line and the Asuras to form another, assuring all that they would receive a spoonful of the life-giving liquid. The truth is, Mohini, the enchanting form of God, had no intention of giving amrita to the Asuras. Because they were opposed to the preservation of life, it would have been a disaster if the rebellious Asuras became immortal. Mohini began to pour a little of the nectar into the mouth of each Deva. One of the Asuras disguised himself to look like a Deva and sat in line between the Sun and the Moon.

Just as Mohini poured Amrita into the Asura's mouth, the Sun and Moon spoke up to reveal the deception. The Asura then appeared in its true form as a fierce dragon. Immediately, Mohini drew forth a weapon, which was a brilliant disk of light, and cut the Asura into two parts. Because that Asura had drunk the life-giving nectar, both parts remained alive as a head and a tail. Those parts were named *Rahu*, the head of the dragon, and *Ketu*, the tail of the dragon. Because the Sun and Moon revealed the Asuras scheme, the dragon has been at enmity with them ever since. The shadow of the angry dragon obscures the two great lights, causing eclipses of the Sun and Moon, in an attempt to remove their light.

In this revealing story, the basic conflict of the universe is revealed. In the world of matter, there are two kinds of beings. One has dedicated its free will to the service of God's purpose; the other creates disturbance to the Divine order by excessive selfish desires. The Devas are given immortality to protect them as they maintain order in the chaotic realm of matter. Later, the Asuras were given wine as a substitute for the divine amrita that they were denied. We live between those two extremes. You seldom meet someone who is completely against the will of God or completely committed to the service of God.

Almost everyone is in between the light and the shadow. In that intermediate area we are subject to the control of the Devas and receive reaction for our actions whether we wish it or not. On the microcosmic scale, the Devas are the system integrity which unites our biology and preserves our life. The Asuras or various disturbing conditions are constantly threatening our life. Unknown to us, the Devas of Divine Intelligence are constantly digesting our food, cleaning our waste and restoring our life. On a planetary level—for the Earth is also a being—climate and natural resources are either being preserved and kept in balance or exploited and used selfishly by those with asuric intent.

Amrita, the Secret of Immortality

Amrita is a most meaningful Sanskrit word. The root is *ritam*, which means *the underlying laws of the Cosmos that hold it together and maintain life*. One who violates those unwritten natural laws receives *mritam*, or *death*, as the result. In other words, our improper use of free will in the context of matter leads to premature death. The Asuras are tamasic and the Devas are sattvic. Failure to observe natural law leads to death. The negative prefix—*a*—means *negation. Amritam is the negation of death through the life-restoring liquid of grace*, which flows down from God and is directed to those who wish to live as Devas. Immortality is the gift of going beyond the grasp of karma. The cycle of birth and death and laws of matter cannot affect one who has become a Deva.

A good way to envision the planets is as external embodiments of centers of activity and influence within us. To continue the metaphor with color, at first there was only light and dark. Then from light, the seven rays of the color spectrum emerged: violet, indigo, blue, green, yellow, orange, and red. Those seven represent a further differentiation in the elaboration of matter in the universe from the simple to the complex. By mixing those seven colors, millions of colors are created. If you want to understand the creative process through color, you must understand the seven secondary and then the three primary colors.

The Seven Planets Within Us

To understand astrology, try to understand the next differentiation of natural energies as seven centers of activity, which we use in our everyday life. Remember that we are the same as the Cosmos in all fundamental ways. Now we are going to give a name to the functions in us that are associated with the seven planets.

. The Sun represents the self, identity and the center.
. The Moon is receptivity, nurturance and the mind.
. Mercury is intelligence, discrimination and communication.
. Mars is power, dominance and focus.
. Venus is refinement, creativity and sexuality.
. Jupiter is expansion, wisdom and happiness.
. Saturn is contraction, limitation and structure.

There are many more details for each planet but these are their essential characteristics. Now instead of making this complicated, just ask yourself: which of the seven planets are powerful in my nature? Are you very centered and certain of what you stand for? If so, you are like the Sun or, as an astrologer would say, you have a strong Sun. Are you a person of few words and mostly action, especially the use of force? In that case, Mars is strong while Mercury is less so. Are you extremely nurturing and receptive? Then you are more like the Moon.

In this way you could analyze everyone you know to see how strong or weak he or she is in these seven centers of activity. Most people are weak in several and strong in a few. Some people are strong in all or most. Obviously, those who have many strong planets will be in powerful positions in life with many powerful abilities.

The premise of astrology is: "Whatever you see on the outside can also be seen from the inside." As above, so below. Whatever was visible in the sky at the moment of birth can be read as a blueprint of the gifts that the atma is receiving this lifetime as the result of their previous use of free will. The horoscope, or view of the moment of birth, contains secrets about what, when and how the Devas will bestow the pre-ordained karmic results upon the soul this lifetime. How the atma uses those gifts is the subject of free will and will determine the outcome in future lives. In this way, at any given moment, we have an unseen inheritance coming toward us. The check is in the mail before we receive it. The Devas are the divine postal workers and the horoscope is the receipt of what is being delivered. If you know how to read the language of the heavens, the stars and planets are a blueprint of the structures that have already been decided based on previous actions. As above, so below.

Queen of Evening

We stand obedient to your whim,
O winged princess of the night,
And wait for boisterous day to dim
Your silver spangled robes of white,
Like eyelids, lift the purple edge
Of dusk, whereon the pearled broach,
Your sign, invokes our patronage,
To where you sit in heaven's coach.
The diadem above your brow,
Seven sisters, one of whom is shy,
Your heart, sweet Venus, rising now,
Throbs softly in the azure sky.
And like a corral set with stars,
The fiercest warrior stands demure,
Held in check, the deadly Mars,
Looks on with noble Jupiter.
Enraptured by your countenance,
The playful messenger, in glee,
Excites our minds to sing and dance,
The faint but clever Mercury.
While Saturn looks the other way,
Limping beyond the turning rim,
Ashamed to see such clever play,
Aware that none will play with him.
The wind, your handmaid, starts to whirl,
Tossing blossoms from the trees,
Which, like your tresses, wave and curl,
Your fragrance hovers on the breeze.
O Queen of Evening, full of grace,
We watch you move in royal state,
Gaze upon your smiling face
And yet remain insatiate.

Jeffrey Armstrong

Chapter Thirteen

The Horoscope
A Polaroid Moment of Your Karma

The horoscope is a photograph of the circle of sky at the moment of your birth as seen from the place of your birth. Latitude and longitude can locate where you were born on Earth. Every location is so many degrees east or west of the Greenwich meridian in England and so many degrees north or south of the equator. Earth revolves on its axis once each day. As it does, all the stars in the 360º circle of the zodiac appear to rise in the east, move overhead and then set in the west. That is what we see on a clear night. In fact, the stars, planets and Moon rise and set along the same path followed by the Sun each day. That path is actually the ecliptic, which is Earth's path around the Sun.

This means that at any moment during a 24-hour period, the celestial bodies occupy a certain place in the sky. Just as the Sun is in the east at sunrise, overhead at noon, in the west at sunset or below us at midnight, the planets and stars rise and set throughout the day. Go outside and observe the sky as a circle that surrounds the entire Earth. From horizon to horizon is half the circle; the other half you cannot see. Then if you draw a line from directly above you to directly below you, the sky is divided into four equal parts. Now divide each quarter into three equal parts. This produces 12 permanent divisions of the space surrounding Earth. Astrologers call these twelve divisions the *houses*.

The first house is the sunrise point, due east. The seventh house is the sunset point, due west. The tenth house is directly overhead and the fourth house is below the Earth. If you were born at sunrise, your Sun would be in the first house. If you were born at sunset, the Sun would be in the seventh house. At noon, the Sun would be overhead in the tenth house. Behind the Sun, there would be a group of stars, a sign of the zodiac. Remember that this is the point of difference between a Western horoscope and a sidereal, or Vedic, one. The Western astrologers no longer use the stars' correct positions. In a Vedic horoscope, you would see the actual group of stars in the background behind a planet. In order to create the horoscope, astrologers use the time and place of your birth. From these, they can calculate and see which of the twelve signs is rising in the east at the birth moment. That sign is then in the first house, the rising sign.

As an example, let us use March 21st, 2000, 6:00 am, San Francisco CA, USA. Because of the precession of the equinoxes, we now know that on that day the Sun is not in Aries; it is in Pisces. Astrologers find that information in a book called an ephemeris. An ephemeris gives the positions of the planets in the signs for each day. If you use a Westerrn astrological ephemeris, subtract 23° from each planetary position to get the sidereal, the actual, position of the stars. Nowadays there are computer programs which make calculating the Vedic chart quite simple. At 6:00 am on March 21st the star group Pisces is rising in the east and the Sun is also there. An astrologer now knows which of the twelve houses the twelve signs occupy. Remember that houses are simply sections of the sky. The signs are the twelve groups of stars: Aries, Taurus, Gemini, Cancer, Leo, Virgo, Libra, Scorpio, Sagittarius, Capricorn, Aquarius and Pisces. Those signs always occur in the same order. If we know that Pisces is rising, then Aries (now the second house) will rise next and then Taurus and so on.

What Sign Is Rising?

Since there are 12 star groups and 24 hours in a day, each group remains on the eastern horizon for approximately two hours. A person born at 6:00 am on this day will have Pisces rising. Two hours later they would have Aries rising and then Taurus. On this particular day the Sun is also in Pisces and so it is in the first house. Just as the Sun is in a sign at any given moment, so are the other planets. Each planet moves at a certain speed as it moves in its orbit around the Sun. From our vantage point on Earth it appears that they move through a group of stars at a particular speed. The Earth circles the Sun in a year, so the Sun stays in each of the twelve signs for thirty days. The Moon moves much faster, circling the Earth once every twenty-eight and a half days. The Moon spends only 2½ days in a sign and then moves to the next. Jupiter takes 12 years to orbit the Sun, so it stays in a sign for about a year. Saturn takes twenty-eight and a half years for one complete cycle and thus takes 2½ years to complete one sign.

On the day in question, Jupiter is at 13º, Saturn at 20º and Mars at 5º in the sign of Aries. Since they move at very different speeds, their association in that sign will not last many days. Mars is the fastest of the three and will move into Taurus in a few weeks. But on this day they are all together in Aries. After the Sun in Pisces rises for two hours, Aries will rise. The person born on March 21st, 2000 at 10:00 am will have Sun in Pisces, Aries rising, with Jupiter, Saturn and Mars in Aries also rising, or in the first house. In the morning of this same day, the Moon is in the sign Virgo.

That means while Pisces is rising, the Moon is in Virgo (which is opposite Pisces) and just setting. Visually, you would see the Moon setting in the west as the Sun rose in the east. The Sun is in 7º of Pisces, while at 6:00 am the Moon is at 24º of Virgo. That means this day is just after Full Moon (when the Sun and Moon are 180º apart). In fact, by 10:30 pm of the same day, the Moon moves forward into Libra. At 10:30 pm, later in the evening, Libra is rising with the Moon also in Libra. Since Libra is opposite Aries, on this day at sunset you would see the stars of Libra rising in the east with the Moon nearly full. Setting in the west, you would observe Jupiter and Mars in the star group Aries, with Saturn also faintly visible.

Thus, in the course of one day, there are twelve possible charts based on twelve possible rising signs. Of course, the charts from minute to minute would be different in small ways as each of the planets move slightly. The reading of a chart can be extremely complex at some levels of calculation. To simplify the chart, think of the 12 houses as each having a particular significance. They each represent certain areas of life experience. Then think of the 12 signs as each having particular qualities. Then remember that each planet is connected to centers of power in our being.

Karma Is Shown by the Chart

Now we have the beginnings of a language of significance that can be used to talk about the effects of past karma upon specific areas of life in the current birth. That is what an astrologer attempts to do with the horoscope, to scope out the present impact of past and now hidden actions. In our sample chart, the individual born on that day has the Sun in Pisces for certain. Whatever the Sun represents is modified by the stars of Pisces at that moment. Throughout the day, the Sun is in the 1st, 12th, 11th, 10th house and so on. Sun in Pisces in the first house is a different pattern of destiny than Sun in Pisces in the 10th or 7th or 4th house.

I know it is a stretch for the mind to believe that the Cosmos can be a source of intimate details about what is destined to transpire in our lives. It is amazing that the Devas are continuously active in our lives despite our inability to directly see them. Nonetheless, that is the conclusion of the seers and sages who have handed this divine science of astrology down to us for thousands of years. God the Astrologer does have a plan for us and the details are partially visible in the patterns of light at the moment of our birth. An astrologer looking at these patterns can predict future events and the patterns of karmic unfoldment.

Ten Thousand Visions of
Her Delight

Four days, thirteen times a year I abandoned life,
Four years out of thirty I slept alone,
Sleeping on the bank of the Red River, my wife,
Ruled by the Moon until she became a crone.
For thirty years Saturn toiled, revolving only once,
The silver sundial clocked my days and nights,
Four hundred times she dressed and
shed her veil of months,
Ten thousand visions of her delights.
Fifteen breaths per minute expand to
four hundred per hour,
Ten thousand births and deaths every day,
Four seconds, four seasons furnish illusions power,
Slow it down to two and find the way.
At one breath per minute the veil is
finally rent apart,
Four plus three plus two plus one is ten.
Open now the Sun, which is an eye
within the heart,
The two becomes a zero once again.

Jeffrey Armstrong

Chapter Fourteen

Horoscope and Body Type
God's Secret Revealed

It wasn't very long ago that the British ruled Bharata (India) as a colonial possession. Part of that dominance was an imposition of British law and culture upon the previously existing Vedic culture. In some instances, the British may have improved conditions by introducing new views and practices. They speeded Bharata's entrance into the modern world, which was necessary, but in the process much that was valuable in the culture was threatened or damaged. Ayurvedic medicine was one science that was seriously injured.

Like most moderns, the British simply assumed that Ayurveda was primitive and superstitious, so they made it illegal. This forced the science into hiding as the private property of certain families. With Ayurveda in hiding, its natural connection with Vedic astrology was made obscure. Even now, the schools of Ayurvedic medicine in Bharata are removing Sanskrit and astrology from their curriculum under the pressure of overly materialistic modern scientific thinking.

Originally, the Ayurvedic doctor and Vedic astrologer worked hand in hand to heal any diseased conditions in their clients. Doctors were trained in recognizing the symptoms of lifestyle and bodily imbalance. Using pulse diagnosis and other subtle methods, they were able to analyze the flow of energies in the body and understand their meaning. Vedic astrologers were used like an x-ray machine. Utilizing the horoscope, they were able to look within and into the future to understand the timing and release of karmic reactions affecting health. Both were looking at the same reality with their respective tools.

In my journey of learning over the last thirty years, I have had to piece many of these understandings together from evidence of past practices. For the most part, books on Ayurveda did not describe the horoscope of the patient and books on astrology did not describe the exact correlation between the horoscope and body type. You might say the whole field is in a state of historic disrepair. It is no wonder, after being ignored disparaged and underfunded for so long.

My journey of discovery led me to examine these connections very closely. Anyone who is trained in the modern scientific method, as I have been, has the habit of examining everything to determine its objective qualities. Since our mind can easily project its thoughts as if they are objective physical truths, modern science has been a struggle between our powers of imagination and objective truth.

Conversely, anyone who is trained in the yogic and spiritual science of the Vedas is comfortable following the imagination back to its source in the ultimate place of Divine origin. One skill requires that we go within to connect with our inner self and the inner source of our consciousness and true being; the other demands extremely precise and objective observation of the outer or physical world.

Remember the question "Why is an intelligent fellow like you an astrologer?" The answer: With the birth information of a complete stranger I can tell you about their parents, partners, sex life, occupation, intellect, passions, abilities, energy levels, health problems, financial situation, good and bad habits, level of honesty and integrity and truthfulness! The list goes on. If karma is real, our body and mind are the repository of the past, present and future events that we have generated. We are the record of our past, and the future is partially an echo of our past actions.

Think of our past actions as encoded within us like a barcode. All you need is a barcode reader to access the information. So-called psychic ability is nothing more than being endowed with a karmic barcode reader. Some people are born with the ability, others develop it through spiritual and yogic practices. Vedic astrology is another method of accessing that database of karma. In fact, almost every culture has developed a tool for accessing this hidden karmic information. I Ching, tarot, runes, tea leaves, sheep entrails, and many other media have been used with varying degrees of success as data collection devices for psychically developed adepts.

What is remarkable about Vedic astrology is that it has been used scientifically for thousands of years to observe karmic patterns. Libraries of information have been collected and exist in India in the Sanskrit language. But I asked myself: "What is the most obvious and consistent thing the chart reveals?" If the horoscope is a representation of the individual's complete physical and mental being, it must correlate directly with the body type. If not, why would the ancients use the same five-element language in both Ayurveda and Vedic astrology? This is where the tires hit the pavement.

What I rediscovered is the most obvious, scientific, physical and most useful connection. For a moment, forget all the other karmic information. The most basic and visible point is that our body type is completely predictable from the Vedic horoscope. I can demonstrate this to anyone. It is easy to see and scientifically verifiable. I call this profound connection AyurVedic astrology, predicting the body type from the horoscope. This is the proof before our very eyes that God the Astrologer has a plan for us, which was written in our horoscope at the moment of birth. At the birth of a child you can predict its adult body type. This proves that God is fashioning us out of the five elements and three gunas and even allows us to see his work through the horoscope.

The connection between the horoscope and the body type is only possible with a star-based astrology like the Vedic system. The body type correlation does not work with Tropical astrology since the correct star positions are not used. With a Vedic horoscope it is possible to accurately predict the body type without seeing the person. Remember that the five-element building blocks are the basis of both systems. In my own pioneering work as a Vedic astrologer I am almost always able to predict the body type of the client whose birth information I have been given. Someday when there is funding for such research, it will be very easy to scientifically validate this correlation.

Imagine the Possibilities

On the subject of proving astrology, I have given this a great deal of thought over the years. The well-funded scientific critics of astrology are always saying that astrology is unable to stand a scientific test. Well, I would like to propose a simple test. Give any group of scientists in the world the birth information of one thousand randomly chosen subjects and a personal computer. Give me or any qualified Vedic astrologer the same information and tool. Then ask each of us one hundred specific questions about each person and see who gets the most right answers, the scientists or the astrologers. If I had a million dollars, I would put it up as a prize for this contest. Perhaps there is a wealthy patron somewhere in the world that would like to sponsor this historic test. We could use a million dollars to pay for some progressive Ayurvedic medical and astrological research.

Think about the possibilities. What if all the previous sages and thinkers are right? What if Nature builds our bodies and minds in visible and predictable ways? What if you can see at birth the diseases, transformations and events and timings that were previously created by a person in their previous lives? Imagine the correlations with genetics and medical research. Think of the implications in education. Would it not be better to educate a person in harmony with their established tendencies? In Bharata, it is still the custom to consult a Vedic astrologer before getting married, while suffering from chronic medical problems, when a child is born or at the beginning of any new venture.

Compatibility

On the subject of compatibility, has our scientific civilization come up with any brilliant methods of compatibility analysis? The last I heard the divorce rate is at about 60%. That is worse than chance! You could flip a coin and get better results. Vedic astrologers have practiced marriage compatibility for thousands of years. Through the horoscope, they can identify energetic patterns and many tendencies that will only show up later in life. Most relationships are simply based on physical or material attraction, but for marriages to last they need to be based on more enduring levels of compatibility. In fact, there are five distinct levels of compatibility, but I will save that for another book.

Astrology Can Time an Event

Another sub-science within astrology is timing of an event. Think about it. If the planets and stars are emanating cosmic rays which then strike us on Earth in specific patterns depending upon where they are in the sky, wouldn't that be a good thing to know? If you were launching a space shuttle, would you like to know the weather? How about whether or not sunspots were occurring on that day? What if an astrologer could predict the hourly variations in cosmic energy and understand which pattern is beneficial to which kind of activity? If this was four hundred years ago, you might just tell me this astrology stuff is all invisible fairy dust and burn me at the stake. But now we really do know better. For all my frustration with the insensitivity of mechanistic science, I have to give them credit for proving the existence of invisible cosmic forces. In spite of great resistance, astrologers have been pointing to those invisible forces for thousands of years. The truth is, science just keeps finding smaller and subtler forces in Nature and it appears, even empirically, that everything which exists is connected at a speed beyond that of light. Even two hundred years ago, the only people talking like that were astrologers!

How Does This Affect Our Daily Lives?

Now let us take a bigger look at the implications of the mind/body relationship by extending an understanding to our ongoing relationship with the Earth and the celestial forces in the sky. The continuous unfoldment of material manifestation on Earth is always in the context of seasonal cycles. Each geographic location has a particular seasonal unfoldment that is really the interplay of the five elements. Each climate will cause predictable effects on each body type. If you are a pita, or fire, type and live in a hot climate, you run the risk of overheating. If your diet consists mostly of heating foods and alcohol, a fire imbalance would be likely. From noon until three in the afternoon, especially in summer, the pitta effect would be dangerous. Those are the terrestrial, dietary and climatic influences.

In addition, the cosmic energies of the stars and planets are always recombining as they move. Those combinations also release energies that finally manifest as one of the five elements. This could add to the imbalance. On an even subtler level, layers of seedling karma could fructify at a particular time, which would trigger mental attitudes, which would in turn influence the development of the physical body. In this way, many observable energetic variables are affecting us at any time, far more than we can understand.

Seasons and celestial influences affect each person according to specific combinations of elements of which they are composed. Vedic astrology is also called the *science of time*, since it reveals the growth patterns of karmic seeds stored within the soil of our mind and body. Without the obvious five-element interface, detailed and complex theories of modern science are doomed to remain the property of a privileged class who can afford the machines necessary to use them. In that way, modern science is a disempowerment to most individuals. If Vedic astrology, five-element science and modern scientific methods are properly blended, we may develop a science useful to every person for preventing imbalances and ultimately disease.

Another Universe

It is as if my head is in another universe,
My consciousness is not engrossed,
My heart can see the lies,
My eyes can see the lines.
Cracks in the well wrought illusion,
I smell the glue that holds it.
I see the elements apart,
Fire, water, air, space,
Earth is not my starting point
Hell, I'm barely here,
Held by a few silver threads,
Mind, intelligence, ego,
None of this belongs to me.
This puppet show of names and forms,
Hologram in space, I see the code
Line by line refresh the screen,
Moving pictures, the plots and themes,
A dime novel, God's soap opera
And now a word from our sponsor:
"Passion turns this Ferris Wheel,
Jaded hucksters, games of chance.
Step right up, win a birth in paradise,
Try your luck." The suckers blink.
Bright lights, the deafening roar,
A constant flame the corpses burn.
I stand on my own shoulders,
Looking over a wall of black
And I see divine gardens,
Stretch into infinity.

Jeffrey Armstrong

Chapter Fifteen

Ego Fills the Space Not Filled with Knowledge

When we are born, our future is a complete unknown to us. That does not mean we do not already have a future, but our experience is that we only know the present. From our point of view, being a baby is a very humiliating and vulnerable experience. As a soul, we do not appreciate the limitations of old age or extreme youth. As a baby we are a cute but ignorant bundle of ectoplasm, spending our time eating, sleeping and evacuating—not a very exciting time in our life. Not long ago I saw a T-shirt that summed it up very well. It read: "I pee, I poo, I drink my moo. I'm a baby—that's what I do!" During that vulnerable time we develop our first mechanism of survival, the "EGO".

The "I-am-my-body" consciousness is our first strategy of survival. At that point you could say we are selfishness and egotism personified. None of us arrive with a "user manual" for planet Earth in our crib. We are born in to a world that is governed by strict cause and effect yet without a clue as to how it all works. Our first response to that ignorant and vulnerable position is to puff up our ego and bluff our way through anything we don't know. "Fake it until you make it" is our motto.

How the Soul Is Held Hostage

Of course, I am not suggesting there is anything wrong in this. Ego or bodily identity is the integrating principle which manages the necessary boundaries of our physical being. The problem arises in the soul's dilemma at finding itself overwhelmed by matter. Matter is unconscious compared to us and thus has a dulling effect upon our original intelligence. You could say that we have two kinds of individuality while we are manifesting in the world of matter. There is our core self, the atma, which is our eternal identity. When we enter into the temporary realm, that identity gets lost. It is replaced by a temporary bodily experience, which is our ego identfying with our current body. That body is concerned with defending its own boundaries that are by definition a limitation. This gives rise to the immune system which attacks any apparently non-self thing which enters its perimeters. Ego sets up a boundary in order to create a body for us. Then that same ego creates a police force to maintain the system integrity. All this is required for maintaining the physical self.

The problem is the soul is held hostage, drugged and unconscious, somewhere in a dungeon, in this palace built by ego. She ate the poisoned apple of matter created by the witch of ignorance and is now unconscious of her full potential, waiting for the kiss of the Prince who can awaken her. The problem is not the palace but rather that the real purpose of the eternal self has gotten lost in the process of building the palace. It then appears to us that maintaining the body is the purpose of life. This is how we begin our lives, asleep to our true nature. Some people remain in that sleep for their entire life, dreaming in an illusioned condition of self-forgetfulness.

The "How" and "Why" of It All

I describe that condition as: "Ego expands to fill the space not filled with higher knowledge." Just as there is an eternal self and a temporary ego constructed of matter, there are also two kinds of knowledge: "why" and "how". "Why" knowledge is about why the palace of ego was built in the first place. It asks the question: "Who am I really and what is the purpose of life? Is there a higher intelligence and where do I go after the death of the body?" "How" knowledge asks about the laws that govern matter. This is the domain of material science. The investigation of how matter works is natural and eventually leads to asking "why" questions, if it is conducted honestly.

Our problem at birth is that we are in a strange and unfamiliar atmosphere with no survival skills. Our first impulse is to cover our ignorance with plenty of ego and then learn the "how" knowledge of survival as quickly as possible, so that life is less threatening. The knowledge of how things work gives us power over matter and makes us feel more secure, but it also strengthens our ego. Right now our world is suffering from an "expanded ego and how-knowledge imbalance." We are out of balance with Nature and underdeveloped in understanding the why of our existence. The so-called primitive cultures which preceded us often were as advanced in the "why" knowledge as we now are in the "how" information.

Vedic astrology is connected to the "why" knowledge and is a bridge into the world of "how". The horoscope is a blueprint of the current ego-built mind-body system. The map of the heavens at the moment of birth is as complex as our genetic code. Though few astrologers can read it at that level of complexity, it is still a useful tool for seeing otherwise subtle or invisible relationships of cause and effect between our past action and present results. Since we are eternal, without looking at cause and effect from life to life, we do not really see the big picture of what is happening.

Our Ancestral Boundaries

Another way to think of our dilemma is to envision our ego as originating from our ancestral limitations. Our genetic material is the result of the qualities and experiences of the generations that preceded us. The body we develop is related to the ones they previously had. In this way, family also is both an advantage and a limitation. If you define yourself in terms of family, the circle of family simply becomes the extended boundary of your ego. You would think: "My family is self and all others are not self." That is extended ego. If you extend the circle further, it becomes your tribe or village, then state, then country, then planet. But as long as you define yourself in material terms, that is a limitation upon the soul. From the spiritual point of view, we do not have nationality or gender or family in the material sense. Unfortunately, that understanding has mostly gotten lost. In its place, modern ways of thinking have filled us with more complex versions of our material self. Filling the space with ego or excessive knowledge of matter is not a real answer to our needs.

The way this works in our daily life is really quite problematic. How we view our material boundaries is the core issue of all human relations. In all social situations we are challenged to deal with many other beings, most of whom are also in forgetfulness of their eternal self. That means they are identified with the material body and the conditioned mind. In other words, they are misidentifying with the five elements and three gunas of which their body is made. You could compare this state of confusion to driving in a car and then imagining you are the car.

To make things more difficult, the ego has activated the immune system to respond to anything which appears a threat to the safety of our physical being. And since our mental being is tied to the body, we can also trigger the immune system by all sorts of thoughts and imaginings. The net result is a kind of mass hysteria that afflicts most human beings. They have no real knowledge of their spiritual identity and, to make matters worse, they have no understanding of how matter is constructed or the laws that govern its actions. They are inexplicably driven to defend the boundaries by which they define themselves. This is as true for countries as it is for individuals. We find ourselves separate and in conflict with others over group opinions about religion, race, nationality and gender. This warfare begins in our homes, extends to our communities and finally results in global misunderstanding and conflicts.

The Five Elements and the Three Gunas in Our Daily Lives

Imagine our ignorance when, as grown-up and supposedly educated beings, we do not know the elements with which we are made, nor do we know the elements of which our food is made. We do not understand the psychological effects of our actions or the operation of our life force. Most people do not really understand the dynamics of their own sexual energy or that of the opposite sex. Is it any wonder that we find other similarly bewildered humans difficult to deal with? In fact, our natural response to this awkward situation is to fill with ego the space that is not filled with knowledge. Of course, since the combined force of many egos exerts a terrible pressure on those in their vicinity, everyone's immune system is constantly being triggered, which keeps them in a permanent state of emergency and stimulates the use of even more ego.

The positive use of the five-element knowledge and the understanding of the three gunas makes it possible to displace the unnecessary ego and consequent immune reactions. Every day we face situations in which we must decide what objects to associate with or to put into our body. Without this knowledge, our decisions are based on arbitrary likes and dislikes, which is usually just a fancy way to say ego or our habit. Without an awareness of our body type, we have no scientific way to proceed in deciding what to eat. The objects that surround us are either sattvic, rajasic or tamasic and are composed of some mixture of the five elements. With this knowledge, we can gain a sense of confidence and accuracy in our choices. This eliminates fear and unnecessary immune responses and prevents imbalances from developing.

In our relationships with people, this is very important. Much of our life we are surrounded by people who are not of our choosing. Often moral decisions and their consequences seem to be an arbitrary matter of personal choice. With an understanding of the gunas, these choices of value become obvious and scientific. When we see those around us as manifestations of the five natural elements, their behaviors can be understood as a natural extension of each elemental nature. This makes us more accepting of one another, which again prevents unnecessary defensive reactions.

This becomes even more critical in our intimate relationships where we spend a great deal of time with one person. You can love someone and yet still be adversely affected by their elements or gunas. For example, if your partner is a fire type, a pitta, then day after day you will be absorbing fire through their association. You can develop a fire imbalance from that contact, irrespective of your love for each other. Similarly, if your partner is addicted to alcohol or drugs, which are tamasic, you will be injured by that imbalance.

Even most religions have let us down in providing the true knowledge of the why of our self and life purpose. Often they have become corporations dedicated to promoting a single viewpoint, sectarian and intolerant. Many become allied with secular political entities bent on social control or the insular self-serving aims of a priesthood maintaining its own parochial position. When this happens, dogma and hypocrisy replace genuine inquiry and the individual is more often told that they are bad, in need of punishment or simply incapable of understanding.

Open-Ended Religion

Many people declare themselves atheistic just to be out of the clutches of dogmatic and repressive religion. They think: "If your dogmatic version of God is correct, I would rather go to hell." If religion became a place of open-ended inquiry into the universal truths of our existence, it would seem even more exciting than material scientific exploration of the unknown. If religion used love instead of fear as its main motivator and taught the eternal nature of the atma as a starting point, people would feel more empowered by religious teachings.

Our Western culture has not favored openness in religion. We have been caught between four great corporations vying for our body, mind, money and soul. Christianity, Islam, Judaism and Material Science have been our options and they have been warring over our allegiance. Like the big four TV networks, they monopolize the airwaves and teach us not inquiry but dogma, sectarianism and often violence. I am sure this was mixed up with good intentions and knowledge, but the point is that they were so intent on the goal they forgot the process. Perhaps they never fully knew the plan. You cannot teach love of God with violence, aggression and suppression.

According to Vedic knowledge, part of that spiritual process is for each person to go into their own heart and have a first-hand experience of the Divine Intelligence and love that are possible. To the extent one is successful in reestablishing an inner self-identity, the relationship to the outer world becomes more balanced. With the additional use of the five elements and three gunas, stability is achieved on the physical plane, which displaces unneeded ego and immune responses. This is healthier for everyone.

Right now our world is ready to explode from unnecessary ego and excess materialism. We must wake up and learn of our eternal nature in a non-sectarian, non-violent way, in order to restore our proper relationship with the larger universe. Vedic astrology is one part of that great mystery, since it brings to our attention the fact that we live in a fully conscious universe which cares about us and is involved in our actions.

The Silver Path

I built my home
Where the flashing foam
Rises up from the emerald sea,
Over waves of brine,
With a curved design,
Like a shell washed up on the lee.
And my bride the Moon
Came to join me soon,
When the house I built was done,
With her starlight maids,
Crystal balustrades
And a stained glass window. The Sun
Swung from North to South
Past the Dragon's mouth
Until the chill of winter was gone,
From the sting of Antares,
Past the horns of Aries,
To the eye of Aldebaran.
Then the warm winds blest
Our seaside nest,
Which rose and fell with the tide,
So we tiled the floor
With albacore
And made wine from the tears we cried.
And we drank all night
From a cup of light,
At a table and chairs of sand,
On an oyster bed,
With a coral head
And driftwood legs in the strand.
As the palm tree's fronds
Waved like magic wands
Above our loving play,
Where the albatross
Flew like candy floss,
Upon the turquoise spray.
Now on full Moon nights,
When my great pearl lights
The sky with her sparkling laugh,
You can find our place
By the line we trace,
On the waves is a Silver Path.
If you fly due East
With your heart released
From the doubts that hold you down,
We've a spare room here,
You can stay all year
But you're not allowed to frown.

Jeffrey Armstrong

158

Chapter Sixteen

Free Will, Action and Ultimate Destination

S o far, we have been focused upon the interconnected areas of knowledge which must be understood in order to grasp the process of cause and effect as it delivers reactions to the souls in response to their actions. First of all, there is an individual who is asking the question. That is the atma, or individual soul. Another term for that being is *sakshi*, which means *witness*. Each of us is the consciousness, or observer, of all the realities that appear both outside us and within. In the final analysis, no one other than our self can validate what we are experiencing.

The Three Components of Perception

Another way to say the same thing is that there are three components to all perception. The first is that which we are observing, which somehow has a distinct and perceivable existence of its own. The second are the instruments with which we perceive. This could be the senses of our body and any instruments through which we perceive, or it could be internal faculties of the mind and intellect. The third component of perception is ourself as the observer. We have experienced the realms of waking, dreaming and deep sleep but at all times it was we, the atma, witnessing these events.

Paramatma Is the Ultimate Witness

According to the Vedas, there is one additional witness to all these experiences and realities. That consciousness, which is simultaneously present as a witness within all beings and thus aware of all perceptions, is the *Supreme atma*, or *Paramatma*. This is God *in the capacity of the all-pervading maintainer of life*. In other words, just as our individual consciousness pervades our own body and is aware of its sensory experiences, so God's awareness pervades every aspect of matter and is fully aware of all actions and perceptions experienced by each of us. This is happening all at once, simultaneously. It is, of course, inconceivable to us that any intelligence could sustain so many simultaneous and distinct tracks of observation. The Vedas tell us that this is just one manifestation of God's total being—Paramatma. God, as the all-pervading intelligent witness, is situated in our heart as a constant companion. It is we who become distracted by the outer realm of matter and lose track of our potential for relationship with Paramatma.

The Two Realms Within God's Being

This forgetfulness is the reason for Vedic knowledge. In the simplest of terms, imagine that there are two realms within the totality of God's being. One is a realm of eternal existence that is not subject to material transformation. In this realm there is no time or space and none of the five elements or three gunas. Imagine for a moment that we come from an area within the totality of God's being where everything is fully conscious and not subject to birth, death, old age or disease. All the atmas there are fully aware of their direct relationship with God. For the moment, think of this realm as the front of God. Think of it as our original home, our place of origin.

Next, picture the possibility of a second area within the totality of God's being which is a large mass of unconscious energy. Think of that place as the back of God. That energy is fundamentally different than us in nature because it does not have consciousness. According to the Vedas, we as individual atmas have the freedom to journey into either of these two realms of God's being. Our dilemma is that we are small bits of eternal consciousness and being that can be overwhelmed and covered over by the vast material energy. For the purposes of our discussion, let's call these two distinctions the *spiritual world* and the *material world*. We are currently living in the material world, which blocks our view of the spiritual world. Here we only see matter and are surrounded by its dull and unconscious energy. It is the realm of matter in which the five elements, three gunas, Devas, karma, time, space and reincarnation exist.

Souls can live in either the spiritual world or the material world. In order to enter the material world, the atma has to be given a material body for its play here. The density of that matter gives us a kind of amnesia, or forgetfulness, of our original home and true spiritual nature. Under that forgetfulness we act in various ways which generate reaction, or karma. The Devas keep track of those reactions and award them to us in successive births. The continuous process of being born and dying and traveling from one place to another in the material universes is called reincarnation. The Sanskrit word for this process is *samsara*, or *the cycle of repeated birth and death*. The implication is that once the atma enters matter, it becomes stuck within its realms of experience. In order to leave the material experience behind, the soul must voluntarily choose to return to the spiritual world.

If we back up and see this process in slow motion, picture the unlimited, innumerable, eternal atmas as they choose to venture into the material world from their original home in the spiritual world. You might well ask why they would venture forth into the material energy and subject themselves to such a difficult process. It certainly is a mystery that is beyond the scope of this book. Suffice it to say for now that something in their own eternal nature makes exploring matter one of the options of complete freedom of self-expression. They choose freely and are then captured by the forces of the material Nature.

This is a little like the birth process. Once a being is inside the mother, barring an abortion, a series of automatic material processes will occur as Nature constructs a body out of the inert principles of matter. Picture the atmas as travelers about to undertake a great journey into another universe. It is as if they are space travelers flying to another galaxy. Before they arrive in their new home, two things will happen: they will be given a spacesuit (a material body) and they will get amnesia to forget where they were previously.

Forgetfulness of Our Original Nature Is Called the Gap

In the Vedas, *forgetfulness of our original self-nature* is called the *gap*. According to Ayurvedic medicine, that gap of forgetfulness of our true origin is incorporated into the structure of our mind. From that point onward until we are reawakened, we experience our self as a separated individual, disconnected from God and others by the boundary of our material body. By the time we grow out of the fog of birth and childhood, we grow up into what modern philosophy calls an "existential dilemma." We perceive ourselves as individuals separated from all other individuals and at war with the laws of Nature that surround us.

In that situation, we use our free will to choose a path of action. We live, eat, think, mate and act as we wish. The trouble is the laws of Nature in the matter that surrounds us are precise and unforgiving in their response to our ignorance. According to Ayurvedic medicine, this is the source of all disease. Because of the gap and our ignorance of natural law, we use our free will to act contrary to the unwritten laws of matter. We then suffer the consequences of our unbalance as disease and suffering.

This brings us to another much-misunderstood Vedic concept, the *guru*. For a moment, think in terms of light and dark. Picture the spiritual world as a realm of light and the material world as a realm of darkness. You can easily experience this by observing that as soon as the Sun is gone, the world is plunged into darkness. In Sanskrit, the *unconscious dark material energy* is called the *gu* (which certainly appears to the atma as a sort of sticky goo). The word *ru* means *who removes*. Therefore, a literal definition of *guru* is *that person who removes the darkness of material self-identification and leads the atma back to its original home in the spiritual world*. In the Vedas, there is no sectarian or cultish implication in the idea of guru. You could say that anyone who knows the way back out of matter to the eternal spiritual realm is a guru. Whoever removes your darkness is a guru. The prefix *gu* is also present in the *gunas,* which are the *ropes of matter* or *goo that binds the atma to the realm of matter.*

The Four Ultimate Destinations

In order to better understand the purpose of the Vedas and Vedic astrology, the actions of the Devas and the meaning of free will, it is necessary to understand the soul's ultimate destination. You could say that representatives of any path of enlightenment are travel agents who through their teachings are selling a travel package. At their conclusion, every path of action or thought leads to a destination of some kind.

From where we stand in the midst of our journey, we are always trying to decide where to go next. Wherever you are right now, you cannot stay there. Material nature will not allow it. To

163

be human is to have an acute sense of the fact that we are going to be forced to move on. Similarly, you cannot take anything with you. Even the wealthiest will leave this world naked. Day-to-day life is a series of choices about where to go and what to do next. If you make a wrong choice, danger or death can easily be the result. Every action is based on the belief or assumption that we are moving toward a destination. Therefore, if you can understand the stated or tacit destination of a spiritual teaching, you can understand where the travel agent is proposing to take you.

The First Destination Is Matter

There are far fewer ultimate destinations than there are travel agents. In order to explain the Vedic path and place of Vedic astrology in that vision, I will identify four main destinations. If you examine all the traditions of world learning carefully, it is certain you will find one of these four destinations as the "bottom line" of where you are going as an adherent of any one. The first conclusion is that we are matter. In this view there is no other realm than the one we are in and we are merely a product of matter. There is no God, nor is there another destination. There is no soul and no self other than the body. When we die, we die. There is no other birth or other destination for the self. There is no purpose in life other than the material experiences we are having. There is no long term karma or cause and effect. Somehow Nature was the matrix of life from which it has all randomly and with no higher purpose arisen. This is the origin of that saying, "Life is hard and then you die." In order to escape sectarian religion, modern science has more or less embraced this view. At the end of the day, this is the "no future" travel agent.

The Second Destination Is a Return to Emptiness

The second path is very popular these days. It argues that we have come originally from an empty state of being and somehow have fallen into the material condition. This view accepts reincarnation but denies the reality or value of the individual self. The followers of this path seek to extinguish all forms of individuality and end up in a condition known as Nirvana. *Nirvana* literally means *like blowing out a candle*. This path does not accept the existence of a God and views the Devas as products of our imagination. The ultimate purpose of this path is to extinguish all individuality and cease both reincarnation and existence. Their slogan is: "Those who speak don't know and those who know don't speak." Right now we experience ourselves as specific individual beings. One of the great decisions before us is whether to believe that individuality continues. This path is certain that in the future state there will be no individual or soul and no God or Supreme Being. This is the "nothing vacation to nowhere by no one."

The Vedas Are Intelligent Transmissions from Beyond Matter

The next two paths are Vedic in origin but are shared by many traditions in various forms. What they share in common is that both of them are beyond the material world. The previous two views are derived from observation within this world. The empty path is a negation of all that is experienced in this world. It essentially says that matter is bad and nothing, which is beyond matter, is good. But the Vedic tradition and various world religions hold the view that in order to get information of what is beyond matter, it is necessary for an intelligent transmission to reach us from the spiritual world beyond the border of matter. In such a case, the information about what is beyond matter descends in the form of a message or messenger sent from

165

the world of spirit to inform us that we have forgotten the true nature of our being and where we are originally from. In the Vedic tradition, there is more specific information about that transcendental realm than is available in any other written tradition in the world. Due to the antiquity of the Vedas (for they are at least ten thousand years old), that Vedic knowledge has been slowly seeping into all world culture for at least that long. Our Western ego likes to claim these as modern concepts.

The Third Destination Is to Merge our Being with God's

The two Vedic views of our ultimate origin and final destination come from beyond the boundary of matter. That means they are not provable in matter in the same way that a material law can be proven. The third destination is a spiritual condition which is totally free of all the qualities and conditions of matter. It is formless and without qualities. In it, all things are made of the same energy that is called in the Sanskrit, Brahman. In colloquial terms, *Brahman* is often called "the white light."

This is the source of the term enlightenment. To return to our source and enter into the Brahman effulgence is the aspiration of all followers of the Vedas. This is the return of the atma back to the realm of light from which it originally journeyed forth. Those who aim to achieve that state are often heard to say: "Aham brahmasmi, I am a being of undivided spiritual nature, one with all that exists." Since even one implies two, this viewpoint is called non-dual. Since everything in the material world is dualistic and temporary, its opposite existence is the eternal realm of bliss and light which is the original source of all. The followers of this path say, "The world is an illusion and Brahman alone is our true nature."

The Fourth Destination Is a
Personal Relationship with God

The last of the four paths is an extension of the path of Brahman. Some followers of the Vedas teach that in the liberated stage, after all material energies and qualities have been shed and left behind, there remains a core self which remains an individual being even in the final state of liberation. In other words, in this view the desire and potential for individuation and personal relationship that we experience in the material world is continued in the realm of Brahman. In this view there are realms or worlds of spiritual activity beyond all influence of matter. This stream of Vedic thought aims at re-establishing our lost relationship with God and God is understood to be the Supreme Person. This makes it possible to continue to experience love beyond the loss of our material persona in matter. In this view, being a loving person is a part of our eternal nature.

Why Discovering Your
Ultimate Destination Is Important

When we remove the layers of matter that cover us, what we find is an eternal person whose individuality is not dependent upon matter. In that liberated condition, the atma enjoys a variety of pleasurable relationships with both God and many other liberated atmas.

At first this all seems distant and unrelated to our daily life. You might think that concepts of the nature of God are a distant reality that is not of immediate concern to how we live in the material world. But day to day and moment to moment we are selecting our next destination. Human life represents the moment in our personal evolution when we have the opportunity to ask very profound questions about the ultimate purpose of life. No matter how beautiful they are, plants and animals do not face such a great choice in who they can become. Their freedom is severely limited by the body they occupy. But we humans can evolve or devolve profoundly in one single life. And because of the mind-body link, we literally become whatever we think and speak.

This means that even our body is being transformed into our thoughts. This is the real basis of yoga and religion. For this reason, the Vedic culture is dedicated to the process of liberating the atma from the ignorance and bondage that arise from material misconceptions of self. In other words, being human is an opportunity to experience the apex of experience in the material world, and it is also an opportunity to extricate ourselves from the material world. In Sanskrit, that process is called *mukti* or *liberation of the atma from matter so it can return to the spiritual world*. The followers of the Veda all agree that we come from a realm of spiritual light where there are no material qualities. If you apply this on a personal basis, it would cause the atma to observe its involvement in matter with suspicion. Obviously, many atmas are lost here in a state of forgetfulness of their true spiritual identity.

So it is that the Vedic culture adopted a slogan to state a larger cultural purpose, "From darkness lead me to light, from ignorance lead me to knowledge, from death lead me to immortality." Thus the life purpose of a Vedic follower is to act in such a way that they can return to the spiritual world after the death of their body. If all karma, or action and reaction, was finished and our desire was to return from whence we came, then that atma would be released from the cycle of birth and death. The Vedic horoscope is like a star-lit electronic scorecard held up at the moment of birth. In its varying patterns of light are encoded the secrets of that particular atma's progress in the elements and the gunas. At a certain point, the souls become eligible or qualified for liberation through their own efforts at attaining their original Divine consciousness. Another possibility is that through association with a true guru, they may adopt the path of liberation and burn up huge amounts of karma through a life dedicated to divine service.

The Fourth Destination Is
Within and Beyond Brahman

That path of service or devotion is the fourth destination. Those who aspire to return to the third path, or Brahman, do so by discriminating between matter and spirit in a very careful process of separating one's self from matter. The term for this is *neti neti*, or *not this, not this*. If we are spirits surrounded by matter, then by observation we can separate our true self from the material coverings. The result would be a detachment from matter and a definition of one's identity as "the same as Brahman." In the vernacular of life, when you hear someone say "we are all one" or "it is all one," they are saying, "we are all Brahman which is not individual and has no form and no distinctions." That philosophy originated in the Vedas. The second path uses a similar methodology, except that their ultimate destination is a void or empty state rather than the positive experience of Brahman. That is the principle difference between Buddhism, Jainism and Taoism, which usually promote the empty state, and the Vedic path, which accepts either Brahman or a Personal God.

The fourth destination is actually "within and beyond" Brahman. Remember that the question of destination is as much about where we came from as it is where we are going. Our origin is also our destination. Do you believe we originate in matter, in the void, or in Brahman, and ultimately return to those states with no continuation of our identity or individuality? Does our unique individual self survive the process of death? That is the core question of life. It is at the basis of justice, truth, individuality, freedom and, most of all, love. *Love is the exchange of voluntary service between two free and consenting individuals for the purpose of their mutual enjoyment.* There is no meaning to love without individuality, equality and freedom. If you take any one of these away, there is no love.

This is the ultimate religious question. There is no doubt that as humans we seek love. The evidence is all around us. It is equally obvious that we fail in expressing love on a regular basis. Which is more real: love or hate, desire or detachment? Those who believe that our ultimate state is dull matter, empty void or the homogeneous light of spirit do not ultimately believe in the truth of love or individuality. Their inevitable message is that individuality, desire, emotion and love are states of illusion to be removed from our nature in the process of enlightenment.

To put it more simply, any path that denies the final existence of the individual self and the individuality of God—both as persons—is an impersonal path of attainment. At the end of the journey we will either still be an individual or we will not. We will still be free or not. And we will still be able to express love or not. By definition, we cannot have anything that is not already present in God, from whom we have come. Therefore, according to the other section of Vedic thinkers, within Brahman is another reality that has both form and individuality. That place is the core of the spiritual world. It exists as a realm full of unlimited numbers of individual souls who are fully enlightened and eternal. In that place the Being of God is always visible as a Person with whom all the residents of that world have an eternal loving relationship. In this view, the material world is a temporary reflection of the eternal realm. Trees, flowers, persons, natural beauty of all sorts are reflections of that eternal realm onto the pool of unconscious matter. According to the Vedas, this is the ultimate meaning of "as above, so below."

Love Is Our Ultimate Destination

Of course, here in the material world we doubt that this is so. It is too far beyond the range of our perception and proof. Indeed, it cannot be proven at all in the sense that something material is proven. This vision is the subject of meditation for souls who are deeply searching for the meaning of individuality and love in life. This is a deep and intimate secret of the culture of Bharata that is usually reserved for initiates of the secret mysteries. This knowledge has been given to us in the West at this time in history to compensate for the great dangers that have been unleashed by modern science.

You see, if love is not true and not our ultimate destination, then surely hate, darkness, emptiness, detachment and destruction will prevail. It is like the Devas who through Divine light regulate and maintain our life. If the light and love of God did not sustain them, surely we would be plunged into a terrible darkness and chaos. We as individuals must finally decide for ourselves whether the universe and its laws are supported by an eternal love and continued individuality or whether life is an unkind joke at our expense. If love is not real and eternal, if it is not our ultimate destination, then surely we are deluded in pursuing it in our daily life.

We Are Eternal Beings
Who Are Always Individuals

On a daily basis we face the certain reality of cause and effect in this material world. That is not optional. We may believe that an irrational and unloving force or a God has cast us randomly into a cruel world. In such a world, justice is a mockery since no one is equal in power or advantage. Maybe this is a "dog-eat-dog world," or possibly it is the world presented by harsh and unloving religions, or perhaps the opportunity of life in this material world is part of a grand and loving Divine plan. In the latter view, God has given us the amazing gift of freedom to come and go between the realms of matter and spirit. What if we are eternal beings who remain individuals in either the spiritual or the material world?

If so, then the gift and responsibility that comes with that freedom manifests as karmic responsibility within the realm of matter. It also gives us the potential to express love to a degree which approaches the magnitude of love experienced by God the Person. What if in the final state of our being, we may even become intimate lovers of God, in love with God, just as we have always wished to be in love here on Earth. *God the Astrologer* is a message from the Vedic culture about how to live our lives. In this world we will always receive karma, or reactions to our past actions. When an inevitable reaction arrives, whether it is pleasing or painful, we should understand that it is always just and loving. In the long run, there is no injustice.

Our Role as Guardians Of The Earth

While we live in the material world, knowledge of five-element science and the gunas is crucial to changing the outcome of our daily life. Our health, relationships, business, in fact all areas of our life will be improved by using sacred scientific knowledge. In the next decades and beyond, profound knowledge of how to live in harmony with Nature will be developed by pioneers who are reviving this ancient wisdom. Acknowledgment of our co-operative relationship with the Devas will bring ecology and our role as guardians of the Earth to a new level of perfection.

Ayurvedic medicine, Martial arts, yoga, tantra, Vedic astrology, Feng Shui, Vastu Shastra and a host of other lifestyle sciences will develop around the five-element model. This user-interface to Nature and an understanding of how food, climate and our body type are intertwined is critical to regaining health and balance. Vedic astrology will assist in marriages, business partnerships, education of children, proper timing of projects and a more universal understanding of ourselves as part of Nature. This is the value of the horoscope. It is a tool of self-analysis far deeper than psychology with which to promote further development of a lifestyle of balance and harmony with material Nature. It is the record of our use of free will and is God's gift of freedom and love.

Throughout this book, I have referred to "sacred science" as compared to "material science." In the terminology of the Vedas, the word for that sacred science is *tantra*. Of course you have heard the word and probably think it has something to do with sexuality. A more correct way to think of tantra is its literal meaning, *to weave*. In the culture of Bharata, the sacred sciences, or tantras, teach all the many ways that the universe is woven together into a web of Divine creative intelligence. Vedic astrology is a tantra. Ayurveda is a tantra. The science of sexuality and the proper weaving of male and female energies are also a tantra. *Tantra* also means *that which expands* and the *Cosmos* itself.

The Male and Female Principle, Mr. & Mrs. God

According to the Vedic vision, the spiritual world is an eternal divine realm that exists forever with no death or decay. That transcendental world, is our original home. It is a place with all the beauties and joys we experience in this temporary world but there they are always fresh and not subject to duality. This world is a reflection of that eternal world into or onto the unconscious material energy. This gives rise to two kinds of Divine knowledge. One branch is tantra. Tantra describes the details of how the material universe is created by both a male and female principle, by Mr. & Mrs. God. Just as we are born in matter as either male or female, so before our appearance, God existed in both a male and a female form.

This is one of the great Vedic secrets, that God is always male and female both beyond and within matter. This universe in which we live is the result of the sexual union of Mother and Father God or God and Goddess. All living beings are descended from that original Mother and Father. In our daily life they are visible before us as the Moon and Sun. They are also manifest as all pair opposite things that combine to make life possible. This divine science of tantra includes the five-element knowledge, the gunas, time, karma, the Devas and the details of how God pervades matter. This sacred material knowledge is meant to empower us to enjoy our life in matter while maintaining a co-operative and healthy relationship with all. Sacred scientific knowledge ensures that we will generate good karma. Good karma translates to happiness and ultimately supports liberation.

The Spiritual World, the Realm of Eternal Existence

The second branch of Divine knowledge is direct knowledge of the nature of life in the spiritual world. At one stage of realization that will consist of an experience of the unified principle of Brahman as the all-encompassing spiritual reality of which we are all composed. At the next level of experience, that undifferentiated spiritual light reveals within its core another place of life where everything is conscious. The Vedas contain extensive and detailed information about that realm of eternal existence. According to that knowledge, God as both male and female is perfectly visible in the spiritual world.

Within that spiritual land that is not matter, another form of individuality is experienced that is the alternative lifestyle to our current use of free will within matter. There we are free in a realm of love, light and beauty that is eternal. Here we live with birth, death, old age and disease while seeing before us the potential of a world of beauty that is always just slightly out of reach. It is a reflection onto the mirror of matter. Thus the Vedas tell us "matter is the dictionary of spirit." Of course, we must learn how to read the book. *God the Astrologer* is only a small introduction to the great Vedic and tantric wisdom and knowledge. This is not only academic or theoretical knowledge; it is enlightening, empowering and critical to our everyday lives. It is knowledge that has descended to us from beyond matter and it is about how God the Astrologer maintains balance and justice in the Cosmos.

The Final Choice

Finally, as atmas, we all have the potential to develop a personal and intimate loving relationship with God. If we don't believe that is so, it will elude us. However, if we desire such a loving relationship, then Paramatma within our heart will be our friend and lover in all circumstances. If we wish, in this very life we can desire to be a Deva and be engaged in direct service to God. If we change our mind from material consciousness and volunteer to serve in that way, God's plan for us will also change. Ultimately, either we will serve the Devas unwillingly as the frustrated and bewildered recipients of our karma or we will volunteer to serve God and co-operate with Natural Law. In that case, God will replace karma with direct service to God and love, while creating as perfect a life in matter as is possible.

Guided by Grace

I built my wings
Out of wax and things,
With feathers from falcons and hawks,
Sewn together with thread
From books I had read,
A collection of ancient talks
On the subject of flying
Past the reach of dying,
Spoken by masters of flight.
I trusted their words
To become like the birds
And fly toward the source of the light.
So high on a peak
I had climbed for a week,
I perched on the edge of a wall,
Above an abyss,
Indescribable bliss,
I leapt and started my fall.
Then the wind with a sigh,
Lifted me high,
Higher and higher I glided,
In a spiral ascent
Of enlightenment,
By invisible fingers guided.
On inscrutable trails,
With my amateur sails,
Like a ship of faith on the sea,
In the vastness of space,
Yet guided by grace,
I flew toward eternity.
Next I dove in the Sun
Where the truth is all one,
Which burned every trace of my past,
I emerged in the dark,
In the form of a lark,
On a tree growing twisted and vast.
As the Moon rose above
Shining sweetness and love,
So I flew once again to its light.
That nectarian globe
Shed her silvery robe,
Standing naked alone in the night.
Then she lifted her hand
As a place I could land
And I dove toward her shimmering breast,
On the Mother of all
I ended my fall,
In her heart I now have a nest.

Jeffrey Armstrong

Chapter Seventeen

God the Astrologer

It is obvious to any careful observer that life is a mystery. Even though the laws of nature are strict and our situation in the material world is fraught with difficulties, there is no obvious answer to our questions. Material science has arisen as our curiosity to penetrate deeper into the mysteries of matter increased. We have created amazing inventions and overcome many obstacles. However, on a global basis we now face seemingly insurmountable problems which threaten to destroy life as we know it. All of this is taking place within the realm of karma through our use of free will and as a result of cause and effect.

On the other hand, every culture on our planet has received some form of Divine revelation regarding the *why* of human existence. It is clear that whatever and whoever God is, that Supreme Being has supported the development of an amazing diversity. That diversity has given rise to many paths of religious or spiritual practice. Often those revelations of some person's contact with God have later been politicized into religious corporations. From where we now stand, there is a global struggle taking place between business corporations acting out of greed, countries acting out of race or nationalism and corporate religion acting to protect old dogmas and traditions. The individual is overwhelmed by all these forces—what to speak of the daily struggle to survive. Never was there a time when universal knowledge was more necessary.

Core Principles of *God the Astrologer*

It was these same pressures that led me to look for answers that are universally valid. There are basically three places to look for answers that will solve this puzzle of our mysterious world. We will either find the answers in the laws of matter, within our own hearts or in the Divine revelations that were given to past generations. Perhaps, ultimately, it will be a combination of all three. I hope you can look objectively at the concepts presented in *God the Astrologer* and examine them as potential tools of universal value. I believe we are all being pushed beyond the limitations of our religion, race, culture or inherited ignorance. To summarize, the following are the bare principles in *God the Astrologer* for your consideration.

1. The Universe is permeated by intelligence and supported by a Divine and supremely intelligent purposeful Being, who loves each one of us and wishes ultimately for our happiness.

2. We are all eternal beings who are just visiting the realm of matter. We are souls having a "human experience" in a place of birth and death. Beyond the death of our body, we will continue in some conscious and individual form. This is the atma, or eternal soul.

3. The material world in which we live is functioning based on underlying laws which we must obey in

order to obtain a happy result from our use of free will. Those laws are the ritam.

4. Those unwritten laws are supported and enforced by conscious living beings who work in the light of Divine consciousness to regulate the inert matter of this world. Those beings are the angels, or Devas.

5. Matter is composed of parts and categories. There are many possible divisions or refinements of this principle. One of the visible manifestations of those elements is the five states of matter—earth, water, fire, air and space.

6. Matter is neither created or destroyed but constantly changes form. Those transformations are conducted by three great principles—or gunas. These are creation, maintenance and destruction. Everything that exists in nature has a guna or energetic state.

7. All things that exist in matter are made of some combination of the five elements and three gunas. That mixed nature can be seen through careful analysis. All bodies have a body type or mixture of elements. What we call life is a mixing of these universal energies through food, weather, bodies and all that exists.

8. Our existence in this world is rooted in both the Earth and in the cosmic energies of space. We stand in between. Those two great realities constantly feed us the invisible energies of the stars, planets, Sun, Moon and Earth. As above, so below. Everything is interconnected. The horoscope is the blueprint of the body and mind.

9. All of these truths are interconnected, interrelated and can be partially observed through a proper understanding of the positions of the planets, stars, Sun and Moon at the moment of birth. This is the handiwork of God the Astrologer.

All of this is inconceivable to our limited vision. Some thinkers, when they grasp the vastness of the material world, lose their faith in a personal and loving God. Some religionists believe in God but are afraid of science or are unable to see beyond the dogma of their particular religion. Some religions have rules from God but no concept of cosmology. In Western and Middle Eastern cultures, astrology has been feared and mistrusted or trivialized as entertainment. What if all these thinkers are partially correct?

What if they are just like the nine blind men touching the elephant? What if love and an unlimited material world are both true? What if God is the original scientist and cosmologist and lives in a separate Divine realm? Why not have it all? What else makes sense of life? There must be justice or all our values are so much nonsense. There must be eternal love or all our experiences of love are empty delusions. There must be interconnections or the exquisite beauty of this artistic world we call life could not exist. Our free will and hence freedom is so immense, so profound, that we can even oppose and ignore all this and deny love, life, truth, justice and God. Indeed, we are co-creators and almost GOD!

We Are Individual Cells in God's Body

God the Astrologer, then, is the supremely intelligent and powerful architect and builder of the world of matter that surrounds us. Not only does God the Astrologer create the Cosmos, God the Astrologer is the Cosmos. In that sense, the total material creation is God's body and we are individual cells within that body.

In the Vedas that form of the Supreme which is the whole material creation is called the Jagat Purusha, or Kala Purusha. *Jagat* means *universe*, *kala* means *time* and *purusha* means *person*. Just as we the atmas have an eternal form which is covered by our temporary material body, so God, the Supreme Person, has taken on a temporary form which is the Cosmos. Yet, unlike us, God is simultaneously present in the spiritual realm in his original form. Like our bodies, that material universe is subject to time, or kala. Time is inevitable and unavoidable and will destroy everything. In that sense, time is also God. Vedic astrology is called *Kala Shastra*, or the *Science of Time*, because it is the study of the actions of God's universal form.

The stars and planets, five elements, three gunas and all universal principles we have covered in this book are, in this view, integrated system processes in the great universal body of God. The problem with this material form of the Divine is the ferocious and all-devouring nature of time. Time is eating everything, destroying everything. This Kala Purusha has often been depicted in the Vedas as having the upper body of a lion and the lower part of a man. This universal form of God is destructive because of its temporary nature.

This is the vengeful God, the God of laws and rules, who exacts repayment to the penny, "an eye for an eye and a tooth for a tooth." This is the God of justice. Certain religions have placed a great emphasis on the rules and laws given by God. In Vedic terms, they are worshipping the ritam, the intelligence of the Divine as it pervades the Cosmos. Ironically, their rebellious child, material science, has left home declaring that there is no mother or father—only rules. Now the study of cause and effect is allowing us to understand and tamper with the formulas of nature. The danger is that we do not understand and thus destroy the delicate balance of life in the process.

Western Astrology Has Not
Presented Itself as Theistic

Rule-based religions and materialistic sciences have historically been opposed to astrology. This is ironic since astrology is keenly interested in the same rules. The problem has been that Western astrology has not presented itself as theistic or believing in one Supreme Godhead. It has been presented as a mishmash of gods and principles that often appeared to be either some kind of magic or the worship of many gods. Fortune-telling astrology is more focused on the trivial details of our ego-driven day-to-day life. Naturally, it is easy to change the focus from the "ritam" to the "me-tam." So theologians, priests and philosophers have often opposed "fortune-telling" as tampering with psychic forces or the free will of gullible people. In the wrong hands, it is exactly that. Nontheless, any great science can be misused and abused.

The science of Vedic astrology displays the actions of the Kala Purusha, the Universe as God, the God of justice or karma. But according to the Vedas, the source of God the Astrologer is God the lover, friend and beloved. This means love is a greater destination for us than justice. Whenever this principle is understood, the desire for the liberation of love becomes very strong. Liberation means the return of the atma to its original home, outside of matter, to the transcendental spiritual world.

Our dilemma, on one hand, is that we have an atheistic material science that only believes in material laws. It has no sense of obligation to a higher intelligence. This thinking is destroying the very fabric that makes life possible. Following this path, we leave a legacy of poison and destruction to future generations. On the other hand, those who believe in a loving or just Supreme Being are often fanatic and fundamentalist. In their haste to leave the world behind, they lay waste to it and do not have the patience to use it with concern for the ritam.

The Ratios That Make Life Work
Come from God the Astrologer

In between is the knowledge of how they are linked and how they work as a co-operative pair. That knowing is present in Vedic astrology and the other sacred sciences. The ratios and formulae that make life in the world of matter possible come from God the Astrologer. To evolve to our highest level, we must learn to love God as the beloved. To work with the world in a sacred way and to co-operate with Mother Nature and Father God, to preserve all that is beautiful, we must acknowledge and work with the Devas. We have the gift of free will. Our souls continually create karma and become caught in unwanted reactions when we forget that creating our own destiny must be in the context of a personal relationship with God, the ultimate astrologer.

The great secret of Vedic astrology is a proper understanding of our free will and eternal individuality. According to the Vedas, our life on planet earth presents us with a time of making choices that will determine our next step in personal evolution. There are two directions for that personal growth, one is away from the material world and the other is to stay within the realm of matter. Inside the material, everything is governed by cosmic rules, or ritam. We may choose to be Devas and cooperate with the laws of the Kala Purusha, or we can oppose those rules and become Asuras who are against the light. These are the personal choices that we face. Karma is the score card for how we play on the field of matter that can be seen in the horoscope. Our other choices have to do with the future of our individuality outside of matter. We may decide to cease acting as an individual and enter into an empty place or void, or we may consciously merge our individuality into the great ocean of eternal consciousness. On both of those paths, we cease to act as individuals. Lastly, we may learn to act outside matter in our soul body, as an eternal individual being. In that spiritual form, we would continue our personal individual existence beyond karma, matter or time.

These are profound personal choices that face each individual. No one can make these choices for us. It is the secret of life that we all now face at this momentous time on Earth. There are so many of us here now; if we continue to act as Asuras, the world will be seriously damaged for thousands of years to come.

The Deeper Secret Is True Love

The deeper secret in all of this is love. True love is a voluntary giving from a state of freedom. Of all these personal choices presented in the Vedas, my choice is to live in this world as a Deva and a lover of the persons of God/Goddess in the spiritual world. The tools of sacred science presented in this book are an introduction to the knowledge of the Vedas. They are part of a user interface to the material world that is meant for aspiring Devas.

Beyond that balanced and preserving attitude toward matter is the potential for an eternal loving relationship with God/Goddess, the true love of our souls. According to the Vedas, outside of matter there are worlds where love beyond our wildest dreams comes true. The choice is ours, for we continue to create our own destiny either as residents of the material world or by migrating to the spiritual world. Perhaps the next step in our earthly evolution is to learn the ability to simultaneously be a Deva and a resident of the transcendental realm—to live with justice in a state of eternal love, to be "in this world but not of it."

Glossary

AGNI – Fire

AHAMKARA – Ego based on identification of self with matter.

AKASHA – Space or ether.

AMRITA – is a most meaningful Sanskrit word. The root is Ritam, which means the underlying laws of the Cosmos, which hold it together and maintain life. One who violates those unwritten natural laws receives Mritam, or death, as the result. That which overcomes death is Amrita.

ASURA – means against the light. This is the opposite of sura, or godly person. An asura is an ungodly or ego-driven person.

AYANAMSA – The correctional figure which adjusts the difference between the Tropical and Sidereal Zodiacs.

AYURVEDA – The science of enhancing and sustaining life.

BHAGAVAD-GITA – The core teachings of the Mahabharata which consists of a conversation between Krisna and Arjuna. It is considered the most concise summary of the Vedic teachings.

BHAGAVAN – A name for God meaning the possessor of all possible great qualities.

BHARATA – British ruled Bharata (India) as a colonial possession. The correct term for the people of India is the residents of Bharat's Varsha. Bharata was a great king thousands of years ago and varsha means land, place or continent.

BRAHMAN – The non-dual reality which includes all reality within its being.

BRAHMA – The creator of the universe.

BUDDHI – Intellect.

DEVA – means playing in the light or the angels or beings who work in the light and serve God by supporting and maintaining Nature.

DOSHAS – The three constitutional components which are composed of the five elements.

GANESHA – Son of Shiva and Parvati and "remover of obstacles."

GRAHA – Planets; means to grab or grasp.

GUNAS – The three states of matter—raja, sattva and tamas—literally, ropes that bind us to matter.

GURU – is that person who removes the darkness of material self-identification and leads the atma back to its original home in the spiritual world.

JALA – Water.

JIVATMA – The individual soul which transmigrates from body to body.

JYOTISHA – The science of Light, the formal name for Astrology.

KALA PURUSHA – The universe as a form or body of God. As we occupy a body, which is temporary, so the universe is seen as a temporary body of God.

KAPHA – Dosha composed of Earth and Water.

KARMA – The results of previous action.

KRIYAMANA – Future karma which is being generated through present action.

MAHABHARATA – The most famous epic of the Vedic Culture. 100,000 Sanskrit verses tell the ancient history of India up to the time of the appearance of Krishna 5,000 years ago.

MAHABHUTAS – The great elements of which the universe is created.

MANAS – Mind.

MAYA – The illusory state of consciousness in which the soul identifies itself with matter.

MUKTI – means returning to our original consciousness which is non-material.

PARAMATMA – That aspect of God which is present in the heart of each being along with their soul.

PITTA – Dosha composed of Fire and Water.

PRAKRUTI – Ayurvedic constitutional type which does not change but can be modified.

PRARABDHA – Karma which is already manifest or which must manifest.

PRITHIVI – Earth.

PURANAS – Supplementary books which explain the Vedic knowledge in story form. There are 18 Puranas: Bhagavat, Vishnu, Garuda, Brahmavaivarta, Varaha, Shiva, Linga, Kurma and others.

RAJAS – The guna associated with creation.

RAMAYANA – The other great Itihasa, or historical epic. This is the famous story of Rama, Sita Hanuman and Ravana.

SAMSARA – The cycle of repeated birth and death which is created by karma over time.

SANCHITTA – Karma which exists in the subtle body in a seedling or unmanifest form.

SATTVA – The guna associated with preservation.

SHIVA – The destroyer of the universe.

TAMAS – The guna associated with destruction.

TANTRA – Knowledge of the functional principles on which the Cosmos is based.

UPANISADS – The Upanishads number 108, though 10 are considered most critical. These are philosophical and esoteric treatises which reveal the details of Vedic spiritual knowledge.

VATA – Dosha composed of Space and Air.

VAYU – Air or wind.

VEDANGAS – The six limbs of knowledge which support the Vedic culture. These include ritual, poetics, etymology, grammar, astrology and medicine.

VEDANTA SUTRAS – This text is the most concise and difficult summary of all the Vedic philosophical teachings. Veda means knowledge and anta means the end of; sutra means thread. Vedanta Sutras teach the end toward which all the strands of Vedic knowledge are moving.

VEDAS – the Rig, Sama, Yajur and Atharva Vedas are the original source of Vedic culture and knowledge.

VEDIC ASTROLOGY – is also called Jyotisha or the Science of Light.

VIKRUTI – The constitutional type modified by lifestyle and diet.

VISHNU – The preserver of the universe.

YOGA – Literally means 'link' or 'combination'. This word has broad implications and is used in many ways throughout the Vedas and within astrology. Primarily, the word yoga refers to the processes employed for reconnecting the soul with its divine origins. For example, bhakti-yoga means to unite with God through devotion, or bhakti. In astrology, yoga refers to various planetary combinations, e.g., Saraswati-yoga—a yoga of planetary positions that indicate that one has the blessings of Goddess Saraswati, the goddess of learning.

Bibliography

Apte, V.S. 1978. *Sanskrit-English Dictionary*, Motilal Banarsidas, Delhi.

Aurobindo, Sri 1959. *The Foundations of Indian Culture*, Sri Aurobindo Ashram, Pondicherry, India.

Barton, Tamsyn 1994. *Ancient Astrology*, Routledge, London, New York.

Behari, Bepin & Madhuri Behari 1975, *Introduction to Esoteric Astrology*, N. Sagar Publications, New Delhi.

Behari, Bepin 1992. *Fundamentals of Vedic Astrology*, Passage Press, Utah.

Berry, Arthur 1946. *A Short History of Astronomy*, Dover Publications, New York.

Bhaktisastri, S.D. 1961. *Sri Chaitanya Mahaprabhu*, Sri Gaudiya Math Press, Madras.

Bhaktivedanta, A.C. 1972. *Bhagavad-gita As It Is*, Macmillan, New York.

Bhasin, Jyotirvid, J.V. 1984. *Astrology in Vedas*, Ranjan Publications, New Delhi.

Bon, H. 1973. *Sri Caitanya*, Oxford and IBH Publishing Company, New Delhi.

Brahmacari, M. 1974. *Vaishnava Vedanta*, Das Gupta & Co., Calcutta.

Chatterji, H.P. 1921. *Sri Narada Pancharatnam*, The Panini Office, Allahabad.

Dutt, B. 1971. *A Review of Beef in Ancient India*, Gita Press, Gorakhpur

Dutt, M. N. 1972. *Vishnupuranam*, Chowkhamba Sanskrit Office, Varanasi.

Egenes, Thomas 1989. *Introduction to Sanskrit*, Point Loma Publications, Inc., CA.

Eisler, Robert 1946. *The Royal Art of Astrology*, Herbert Joseph Limited, London.

Fagan, Cyril 1971. *Astrological Origins*, Llewellyn Publications, Minnesota.

Frawley, David, 1991. *Gods, Sages, and Kings: Vedic Secrets of Ancient Civilization*, Passage Press, Utah.

Ganguli, K. M. 1975. *The Mahabharata*, Munshiram Manoharlal, New Delhi.

Goswami, T. 1976. *Sri Ramacharitamanasa*, Gita Press, Gorakhpur.

Goyandka, J. 1973. *Srimad Bhagavadgita*, Gita Press, Gorakhpur.

Hall, Manly P. 1975. *The Story of Astrology*, The Philosophical Research Society, CA.

Hanumantachar, C. K. 1961. *Nyaya Sudha Kantakoddhara*, MLJ Press, Madras.

Kalyanaraman, A. 1967. *Aryatarangini, The Saga of the Indo-Aryans,* Asia Publishing House, Bombay.

Levacy, William R. 1999. *Beneath a Vedic Sky,* Hay House Inc., CA.

Maitra, S.K. 1936. *Madhva Logic,* University Calcutta, Calcutta.

Mallik, G. N. 1927. *The Philosophy of Vaisnava Religion,* Punjab Oriental (Sanskrit) Series, Lahore.

Mani, V. 1975. *Puranic Encyclopedia,* Delhi.

Mehta, Harkant M. 1987. *Astrology,* The New Order Book Co., Ahmedabad, India.

Moore, Thomas 1990. *The Planets Within, The Astrological Psychology of Marsilio Ficino,* Lindisdarne Press, NY.

Murti, G.S. 1943. *Vadavali by Jayatirtha,* The Vasanta Press, Madras.

Ojha, Pandit Gopesh Kumar 1972. *Predictive Astrology of the Hindus,* D.B. Taraporevala Sons & Co. Private Ltd., Bombay.

Partridge, Eric 1958. *Origins, A Short Etymological Dictionary of Modern English,* The Macmillan Company, NY.

Powell Robert & Peter Treadgold, 1979. *The Sidereal Zodiac,* American Federation of Astrologers, Inc., Tempe, Arizona.

Rachleff, Owens S. 1973. *Sky Diamonds the New Astrology,* Hawthorn Books, NY.

Raghavachar, S. S. 1959. *Srimad-Visnu-Tatua-Viniranaya,* Rama-Krishna Math Press, Mysore.

Rajaram, Navaratna S. 1994. *Vedic Aryan and the Origins of Civilization,* World Heritage Press, St. Hyacinthe, Quebec.

Rajaram, Navaratna S. 1995. *The Politics of History, Aryan Invasion Theory and the Subversion of Scholarship,* Voice of India, New Delhi.

Rao, Prof. S.K. Ramachandra 1990. *The Tantrik Practices in Sri-Vidya,* Kalpatharu Research Academy, Bangalore.

Rau, S. S. 1936. *The Vedanta Sutras with the Commentary of Sri Madhvacarya,* Sri Vyasa Press, Tirupati.

Roy, P.C. trans. 1956. *Mahabharata,* Oriental Publishing, Calcutta.

Santillana, D. and H. Dechend 1977. *Hamlet's Mill,* David R. Godine, Boston.

Sanyal, N.K. 1933. *Sri Krishna Chaitanya,* Sri Gaudiya Math Press, Madras.

Saraswati, S. 1957. *A Few Words on Vedanta,* Sri Gaudiya Math Press, Madras.

Saraswati, S. 1967. *Sri Chaitanya's Teachings,* Sri Gaudiya Math Press, Madras.

Sarkar, B.K. 1975. *The Sukraniti,* Oriental Books Reprint Corporation, New Delhi.

Schmidt, Robert and Robert Hand 1994. *Claudius Ptolemy Tetrabiblos Book I,* Trans. by Robert Hand - Project Hindsight, The Golden Hind Press.

Seshadri, P. 1949. *Sri Sankaracharya,* The University of Travancore, Trivandrum.

Shamasastry BA Ph.D., Dr. R. 1938. *Drapsa: The Vedic Cycle of Eclipses*, Sree Panchacharya Electric Press, Mysore.

Sharma, Bhu Dev and Nabarun Ghose, (editors) 1998. *Revisiting Indus-Sarasvati Age and Ancient India*, World Association of Vedic Studies, Vaidwara.

Sharma, Girish Chand 1994. *Maharishi Parasara's Brihat Parasara Hora Sastra*, Sager Publications, India.

Shastri, S.N. 1971. *The Wise Sayings of Amatya Chanakya*, Bharati Publications, Delhi.

Sidharth, B.G. 1999. *The Celestial Keys to the Vedas, Discovering the Origins of the World's Oldest Civilization*, Inner Traditions International, Vermont.

Suryanarain Rao, B. 1933. *Sri Sarwarthachintamani*, Motilal Banarsidass Publishers, Delhi.

Thakur, B.V. 1969. *The Bhagavat, Its Theology and Ethics*, Sri Gaudiya Math Press, Madras.

Thakur, B.V. 1971. *Jaiva Dharma*, Sri Gaudiya Math Press, Madras.

Tilak, B.G. 1955. *Orion*, Tilak Brothers, Poona.

Tirtha, B. V. 1964. *Sri Chaitanya's Concept of Theistic Vedanta*, Sri Gaudiya Math Press, Madras.

Valmiki. 1974. *Srimad Valmiki Ramayana*, Gita Press, Gorakhpur.

Vasu, B.D. 1918. *Yajnavalkya Smriti*, Panini Office, Allahabad.

Vasu, B.D. 1974 *Prameya Ratnavali*, AMS Press, New York.

Vasu, B.D. 1974. *The Bhakti-Ratnavali*, AMS Press, New York.

Vasu, B.D. 1974. *The Matsya Puanam*, AMS Press, New York.

Vasu, B.D. 1974. *The Vedanta Sutras of Badarayana with the commentary of Baladeva*, AMS Press, New York.

Vasu, B.D., 1910. *Chandogya, Brihadaranvaka, Isa, Kena, Katha, Prasna, Mundaka, Manduka, Kausitaki, Maitri, Aitareya, Taitiriya Upanisads, with the Commentary of Madhvacarya*, Panini Office, Allahabad.

Index

Devas and, 129
ignorance and, 163
karma and, 110,185
material existence and, 162
responsibility and, 171,182

G
Galileo, 56
Gap of forgetfulness, 162
God
    choice and, 170
    churning of milk ocean and,
        128
    as creator, maintainer, and
destroyer, 94
    diversity and, 180
    justice and, 12, 184
    karma and, freedom from, 115
    male and female form of, 172
    merging with, 165
    as original astrologer, 18
    Paramatma feature of, 103
    path of emptiness and, 164
    personal relationship with,
        166,168,174
    realms of existence and, 160
    scientific knowledge and, 46
    tantra and 173
    universal order and, 116,121
    universe as body of, 127,183
    Vedic astrology and, 110
    as witness, 160
    See also Divine intelligence
Graha. See Planets
Greek culture, 15, 48,84,119
Gunas, 92,179
    association and, 95
    body type and, 183

change and, 92
choice of values and, 153
color and, 95
creation, maintenance, and
    destruction and, 92,94
ego and, 154
karma and, 96
moral values and, 93
pervasiveness of, 95
prison system and, 96
qualities associated with, 95,98
realms of existence and, 161
relationships and, 153
tantra and 173
Guru, 163,168

H
Hinduism, 23
Hipparchus, 49
History
    astronomy and, 29
    lost knowledge and, 14, 45,49,
        127
    medical system and, 79,81
    origin of culture and, 15, 48
Horoscope
    karma and, 186
    body type and, 143
    for March 21, 2000, 136
    houses and, 135
    karma and, 138
    liberation and, 167
    location of birth and, 135
Houses, 134,138
"How" knowledge, 150
Human behavior, 13
Human life, 171

A Note From The Author

*"Astrology is described as a remnant of the gods
whose numinosity can still be felt even in a scientific age."*

Carl Jung

I consider myself a Spiritual Archeologist. In addition to degrees in psychology, literature, history, and comparative religion, I have practiced Vedic astrology since 1973 and have been initiated into the mysteries of Vedic, Yogic and Tantric knowledge by Masters of these traditions. My investigations into the 10,000-year-old mysteries of Eastern science and wisdom have allowed me to unearth a previously buried treasure of knowledge.

Over the past 30 years, it became apparent to me that the ancient Vedic culture is the underlying intellectual and spiritual origin of all Western civilizations. By restoring the correct relationships between various fragmented spiritual disciplines, I was able to recognize the interconnection between spiritual and material science. I have articulated this ancient Vedic wisdom in a contemporary framework that is clear, scientific and concise.

My goal is to revive that lost knowledge and present it as tools of empowerment that we can use every day to create balance in the midst of the great pressures of technology and global culture. I think of this knowledge as an amazing software program that will give us new faculties, insights and potential.

Our generation has grown up studying a myriad of spiritual and self help paths. Fifty thousand people are turning fifty every day and are searching for answers to the meaning of their lives. People are redefining their beliefs by choosing consciously from the entire realm of world culture. I call it the World Beat of the Mind. For some people this is a terrifying concept; for others it is the great adventure.

I offer this book as an opportunity for readers to search for truth, wisdom and knowledge from the perspective of both modern science and the great knowledge of past cultures. I hope you will enjoy it.

"We are not here to work for a living.
We're here to work at perfecting living."

Jeffrey Armstrong

MAHABHARATA

The Greatest Spiritual Epic of All Time

As the divinely beautiful Draupadi rose from the fire, a voice rang out from the heavens foretelling a terrible destiny: "She will cause the destruction of countless warriors." And so begins one of the most fabulous stories of all time. Mahabharata plunges us into a wondrous and ancient world of romance and adventure. In this exciting new rendition of the renowned classic, Krishna Dharma condenses the epic into a fast-paced novel—a powerful and moving tale recounting the fascinating adventures of the five heroic Pandava brothers and their celestial wife. Culminating in an apocalyptic war, Mahabharata is a masterpiece of suspense, intrigue, and illuminating wisdom.

"A well-wrought saga that will be appreciated by Western readers. Highly recommended."—*The Midwest Book Review*

"...very readable, its tone elevated without being ponderous."—*Library Journal*

"...blockbuster treatment...Moves effortlessly, often as racily as a thriller, without compromising the elevated style and diction."—*India Today*

"Its truths are unassailable, its relevance beyond dispute, and its timelessness absolute."—*Atlantis Rising*

"I could not tear my mind away!"—*Magical Blend*

Condensed Version
$19.95 ♦ ISBN 1-887089-25-X ♦ 6" x 9" ♦ Hardbound ♦ 288 pgs.
Complete Unabridged Version
$39.95 ♦ ISBN 1-887089-17-9 ♦ 6" x 9" ♦ Hardbound ♦ 960 pgs.
♦ 16 color plates ♦ 20 Illustrations

RAMAYANA

By Krishna Dharma

A THRILLING NEW RENDITION OF THE WORLD'S OLDEST EPIC

Ramayana is both a spellbinding adventure and a work of profound philosophy, offering answers to life's deepest questions. It tells of another time, when gods and heroes walked among us, facing supernatural forces of evil and guided by powerful mystics and sages.

Revered throughout the ages for its moral and spiritual wisdom, it is a beautiful and uplifting tale of romance and high adventure, recounting the odyssey of Rama, a great king of Ancient India. Rama, along with his beautiful wife, Sita, and his faithful brother Laksmana, is exiled to the forest for fourteen years. There, Sita is kidnapped by the powerful demon Ravana. Along with Lakshmana and a fantastic army of supernatural creatures, Rama starts on a perilous quest to find his beloved Sita.

"A spellbinding adventure and a work of profound philosophy, offering answers to life's deepest questions... *Ramayana* is a beautiful tale of romance and high adventure...Faithfully preserved and passed on in varied forms for countless generations, the *Ramayana* is recognized by many Western scholars as a literary masterpiece. Now Krishna Dharma has provided the English-speaking reader with a superb opportunity to discover and enjoy this ancient and influential classic."
—The Midwest Book Review

"(*Ramayana*) makes for lively reading as a good adventure and love story as well as a guide to spiritual practice .This version breaks up what was originally seven long chapters into smaller, easier to handle units. Recommended for any library in need of a first copy or a contemporary and highly readable rendering of this ancient Indian classic."
—Library Journal

$27.95 ♦ £17.99 ♦ ISBN 1-887089-22-5 ♦ 6" x 9" ♦ Hardbound ♦ 488 pgs. 8 color plates ♦ 10 B&W Drawings

BHAGAVAD-GITA AS IT IS

By
His Divine Grace
A.C. Bhaktivedanta
Swami Prabhupada

The *Bhagavad-gita* is the concise summary of India's spiritual teachings. Remarkably, the setting for this classic is a battlefield. Just before the battle, the great warrior Arjuna begins to inquire from Lord Krishna about the meaning of life. The *Gita* systematically guides one along the path of self-realization. It is the main sourcebook for information on karma, reincarnation, yoga, devotion, the soul, Lord Krishna, and spiritual enlightenment.

Bhagavad-gita As It Is is the best-selling edition in the world!

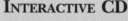

INTERACTIVE CD

Interactive Multi-media CD-Rom version, over 30 hours of Audio, 275 full-color illustrations, video clips, and nearly 1000 pages of text.
$19.95
ISBN 91-7149-415-4.

"*Bhagavad-gita As It Is* is a deeply felt, powerfully conceived, and beautifully explained work. I have never seen any other work on the *Gita* with such an important voice and style. It is a work of undoubted integrity. It will occupy a significant place in the intellectual and ethical life of modern man for a long time to come."
—Dr. Shaligram Shukla, assistant Professor of Linguistics, Georgetown University

"When doubts haunt me, when disappointments stare me in the face, and I see not one ray of hope on the horizon, I turn to *Bhagavad-gita* and find a verse to comfort me; and I immediately begin to smile in the midst of overwhelming sorrow. Those who meditate on the Gita will derive fresh joy and new meanings from it every day."
—Mohandas K. Gandhi

Deluxe edition with translations and elaborate purports:
$24.95 ♦ ISBN 0-89213-285-X ♦ 6.5" x 9.5"
Hardbound ♦ 1068 pgs. ♦ 29 full-color plates
Standard edition, including translation and elaborate purports:
$12.95 ♦ ISBN 0-89213-123-3 ♦ 5.5" x 8.5"
Hardbound ♦ 924 pgs. ♦ 14 full-color plates

BHAGAVAD-GITA
THE SONG DIVINE

**A New, Easy-to-Understand Edition of India's
Timeless Masterpiece of Spiritual Wisdom**

The *Bhagavad-gita*, India's greatest spiritual treatise, contains far too much drama to remain the exclusive property of philosophers and religionists. Woodham presents the timeless wisdom of the *Gita* in contemporary English poetry, bringing to life its ancient yet perennially applicable message. It recounts in metered stanzas the historic conversation between Krishna, the Supreme Mystic, and the mighty warrior Arjuna as they survey the battlefield preparations for the greatest world war of all time. This reader-friendly edition will attract the minds and hearts of not only spiritualists and philosophers, but of dramatists, musicians, children, poetry-lovers, and all who seek inspiration in their daily lives.

$15.00 ♦ ISBN 1-887089-26-8
♦ 5" x 7" ♦ Hardcover ♦ 118 pgs.

THE EYE OF THE STORM

by Austin Gordon, Ph.D

The Eye of the Storm is a concise, easy-to-read synthesis of the perspectives and practices of an ancient culture in the art of developing true peace of mind. Gordon presents a cogent alternative to modern views on the nature of the mind and the self that furthers our understanding of our natural, peaceful psychological condition. This fascinating perspective provides invaluable guidance in freeing ourselves from the anxieties and misconceptions that cover our natural serenity.

$11.95 ♦ £6.99 ♦ ISBN 1-887089-24-1
♦ 5" x 7" ♦ Hardcover ♦ 120 pgs.

Book Order Form

- ◆ Telephone orders: Call 1-888-TORCHLT (1-888-867-2458)
  (Please have your credit card ready.)
- ◆ Fax orders: 559-337-2354
- ◆ Postal Orders: Torchlight Publishing, P O Box 52, Badger, CA 93603, USA
- 🌎 **World Wide Web: www.torchlight.com**

PLEASE SEND THE FOLLOWING:	QUANTITY	AMOUNT
❑ **Bhagavad-gita As It Is**		
Deluxe (1,068 pages)—$24.95	x_____	= $_____
Standard (924 pages)—$12.95	x_____	= $_____
❑ **Bhagavad-gita Interactive CD**—$19.95	x_____	= $_____
❑ **Bhagavad-gita, The Song Divine**—$15.00	x_____	= $_____
❑ **Ramayana**—$27.95	x_____	= $_____
❑ **Mahabharata, unabridged**—$39.95	x_____	= $_____
❑ **Mahabharata, condensed**—$19.95	x_____	= $_____
❑ **The Eye Of the Storm**—$11.95	x_____	= $_____
❑ **God the Astrologer**—$16.95	x_____	= $_____
Shipping/handling (see below)		$_____
Sales tax 7.25% (California only)		$_____
TOTAL		$_____

(I understand that I may return any book for a full refund—no questions asked.)

❑ PLEASE SEND ME YOUR CATALOG AND INFO ON OTHER BOOKS BY TORCHLIGHT PUBLISHING

Company _____

Name _____

Address _____

City _____ State _____ Zip _____

PAYMENT:

❑ Check/money order enclosed ❑ VISA ❑ MasterCard ❑ American Express

Card number _____

Name on card _____ Exp. date _____

Signature _____

SHIPPING AND HANDLING:

USA: $4.00 for the first book and $3.00 for each additional book. Air mail per book (USA only)—$7.00.

Canada: $6.00 for the first book and $3.50 for each additional book. (NOTE: Surface shipping may take 3 to 4 weeks in North America.)

Foreign countries: $8.00 for the first book and $5.00 for each additional book. Please allow 6 to 8 weeks for delivery.